Puppy Raising & Training Diary For Dummies®

Cheat Sheet

Diary Page

Monday

Gave Fido an extra meal today — he's a hungry little guy. Checked with the vet first. I don't want to feed Fido too much, but when he looks at me so pleadingly with those big brown eyes, it's hard to resist.

Tuesday

Walked Fido right after breakfast. Made sure he had enough clean, fresh water in his bowl.

Wednesday

Teach Fido to sit by next week.

Thursday

Played the Squeak Toy Shuffle with Fido today after I came home from work. He really enjoys following me around.

Friday

Puppy Raising & Training Diary For Dummies®

Cheat Sheet

Saturday

All puppies have different nutritional needs. One formula just can't suit everyone. Find out as much as you can about the nutritional needs of your puppy. Talk to your veterinarian, breeder, and educated, pet store professional to find the diet that is more suited to your puppy.

> Worked on "sit" several times today. Not sure if Fido is
>
> totally getting it. Sometimes he seems to know what I mean,
>
> other times he doesn't. Will keep at it.

Sunday

> Worked more on "sit." Fido seemed to catch on more
>
> today than yesterday. I think he's learning!

Tip of the Week

It's okay to feed your puppy some table scraps. Stick to cooked pieces of chicken, turkey, beef or lamb. Avoid all poultry bones, because they can break off and choke your pup.

Wiley, the Wiley Publishing logo, For Dummies, the Dummies Man logo, the For Dummies Bestselling Book Series logo and all related trade dress are trademarks or registered trademarks of Wiley Publishing, Inc. All other trademarks are property of their respective owners.

For Dummies: Bestselling Book Series for Beginners

Puppy Raising & Training Diary

FOR
DUMMIES®

by Sarah Hodgson

Wiley Publishing, Inc.

Puppy Raising & Training Diary For Dummies®

Published by
Wiley Publishing, Inc.
111 River Street
Hoboken, NJ 07030
www.wiley.com

For general information on our other products and services or to obtain technical support, please contact our Customer Care Department within the U.S. at 800-762-2974, outside the U.S. at 317-572-3993, or fax 317-572-4002.

Wiley also publishes its books in a variety of electronic formats. Some content that appears in print may not be available in electronic books.

Library of Congress Cataloging-in-Publication Data:
Library of Congress Control Number: 2001092896
ISBN: 0-7645-0876-8

Manufactured in the United States of America
10 9 8 7
3B/RV/QY/QU/IN

About the Author

The first thing that comes across clearly when you meet Sarah Hodgson is that she's mad about her profession — teaching dogs and training people. For her, it's a life's passion, not a job.

From early childhood, her infatuation with animals and what they were communicating was apparent to everyone. Although she didn't grow up in an animal-centered environment, she soon surrounded herself with all sorts of creatures: from domestic dogs and rodents to wildlife that she rehabilitated. Her first exposure into the dog world was when she began working at a local kennel at age 12. Soon after, she locked into the magic of teaching dogs, and she became a self-proclaimed dog nut. After teaching her own, she went around the neighborhood and offered to train everyone else's dogs.

Sarah entered the pre-veterinarian program at Michigan State University. Although she finished her degree in Biology with an emphasis on Psychology and Animal Behavior, she had already found her life's calling: teaching dogs and training people. At first she trained dogs to earn money through college, but it was clear long before graduation that training dogs was what she loved to do. For her, there was never any other option.

In upstate New York, Sarah has sustained a dog-training school for 14 years. During that time, she has built in her love of writing — completing several training books and serving as a corresponding columnist for *The New York Times*. From 1990 – 1995, she also worked as the press escort under Thelma Boalby, giving her invaluable introductions to those influential and well respected in the dog circles. And the greatest influence on her training methodology came from Job Michael Evans, a former Monk of New Skete.

Sarah continues to teach dogs and train people under the business name Simply Sarah, Inc., in Bedford, New York. In addition, she enjoys participating in public events and media appearances to raise canine awareness. But her favorite time of day is when she takes her own dogs, Hope and Shayna May, hiking in the woods. She says that's as essential to her day as drinking water.

Dedication

For Abigail, Martha, and Philippa Biddle, and all the paws to follow.

Acknowledgments

So many people to thank — I haven't a clue where to begin.

First, hats off and paw up to my agent, Deborah Schneider. Your steadfast encouragement has been a mystery to me but something I could not do without. Dominique, you're my queen! You've been a good friend, great editor, and — *can you believe it?* — one heck of a publisher. And to the rest of my editing staff . . . Nikki, your upbeat wackiness makes writing for you fun; Sandy Blackthorn, alias, "The Saint," I don't know how you do all you do and still remain cheerful; Dr. Amy Rodriquez (D.V.M.), I love you; and Tracy Barr, initials tlb. Thank you all so much.

I can't forget my home team: Laurie Guarino and Louisa Polos, for all your after-school efforts and candid brilliance, and Ridgely Biddle, my final reader. As if you didn't have enough to do!

And of course, to my foundation of friends and family. Two legged and four. If my arms could reach, I'd hug all of you at once.

Publisher's Acknowledgments

We're proud of this book; please send us your comments through our online registration form located at www.dummies.com/register.

Some of the people who helped bring this book to market include the following:

Acquisitions, Editorial, and Media Development

Project Editor: Suzanne Snyder

Acquisitions Editor: Kira Sexton

Copy Editor: E. Neil Johnson

Editorial Manager: Pam Mourouzis

Editorial Assistant: Carol Strickland

Cover Photos: Tim Davis @ Tony Stony

Composition

Project Coordinator: Ryan Steffen

Layout and Graphics: Amy Adrian, Joyce Haughey, LeAndra Johnson, Barry Offringa, Jacque Schneider, Betty Schulte, Julie Trippetti,

Special Art:

Proofreaders: John Greenough, Angel Perez, Carl Pierce, TECHBOOKS Production Services

Indexer: TECHBOOKS Production Services

General and Administrative
> **Diane Graves Steele,** Vice President and Publisher, Consumer Dummies
> **Joyce Pepple,** Acquisitions Director, Consumer Dummies
> **Kristin A. Cocks,** Product Development Director, Consumer Dummies
> **Michael Spring,** Vice President and Publisher, Travel
> **Brice Gosnell,** Associate Publisher, Travel
> **Suzanne Jannetta,** Editorial Director, Travel

Publishing for Technology Dummies
> **Richard Swadley,** Vice President and Executive Group Publisher
> **Andy Cummings,** Vice President and Publisher

Composition Services
> **Gerry Fahey,** Vice President of Production Services
> **Debbie Stailey,** Director of Composition Services

Contents at a Glance

Cartoons at a Glance

By Rich Tennant

The 5th Wave   By Rich Tennant

"I don't think teaching the puppy how to help you cheat at cards was the training and bonding experience the Vet had in mind."

page 47

The 5th Wave   By Rich Tennant

"When we got him several years ago he was a Golden Retriever. Now, he's more of a Golden Recliner."

page 167

The 5th Wave   By Rich Tennant

Beware of Dog

THUNDER

"We're hoping he'll grow into it."

page 5

Cartoon Information:
Fax: 978-546-7747
E-Mail: richtennant@the5thwave.com
World Wide Web: www.the5thwave.com

Table of Contents

Introduction

*W*hether you're starting this book with a puppy curled up at your feet, or you're still in the thinking-about-it stage, welcome. My name is Sarah. Right off the bat — you're not a dummy. You may feel lost and uninformed, *but confusion does not a dummy make*. All you need is some good information to guide you and help you through that first critical year of training and raising your puppy.

About this Diary

So you've decided to bring a puppy into your life. Congratulations! You're in for an exciting time. Puppies are adorable. Puppies are soft and cuddly, and they smell good. But more important, puppies are infants. They require a considerable amount of care and attention, as well as your patience and understanding to help them learn the lay of the land.

Part information source, part motivational tool, and part journal, this book helps you get started raising your puppy and make the most of your training sessions. Yes, it will answer questions that you didn't even know you had when you first met your wiggling bundle of fur.

In these pages, you'll discover how to prepare your family and your home for your puppy's arrival. You'll find out how to teach your puppy his name. You'll get expert advice for housetraining your puppy. You'll discover the joys — and difficulties — of life with your puppy.

In the first chapters of this book you'll also read about the commands Come, Sit, Down, and Stay. In the tips of your diary's pages you'll find more information about these vital lessons. Finally, you'll determine easy ways to resolve puppy dilemmas and train your puppy so that one day he'll be an upstanding young canine.

The most important part of this book is the one that you write yourself. The meat of this book is a customizable raising and training journal in which you can list your puppy's accomplishments, document his veterinary information, log his weight and food consumption, prepare for another week with your puppy, and record the week gone by. This important section makes this book truly *yours*. And finally, because everyone loves a list, the Part of Tens gives you a few more tips and helpful hints.

Why You Need to Log Your Raising & Training Sessions

What logging your puppy's raising and training sessions does is pretty simple. It gives you information *and* inspiration. It demystifies and explains your puppy's occasionally puzzling behavior. It gives you suggestions for dealing with your puppy's difficult stages, namely puberty and adolescence. Did you think that these stages were limited to human teenagers? Well, they're not. Puppies can be teenagers too!

One day, not long from now, you'll glance at the beginning pages of your diary and realize that your well-trained, perfectly socialized, and polite dog once was a confused little puppy. And you'll have recorded his — and your — accomplishments every step of the way.

How to Use Your Raising & Training Diary

The first thing you need to use your training diary is time. The second thing you need is a pen or a pencil. Find one? Great! The next thing you need is a plan. Before you start your raising and training diary, have a general idea of what your puppy raising and training goals are and how to achieve them.

Puppies need to know certain essential things to become good canine citizens. All puppies need to know their names. They need to be housetrained and properly socialized. For safety's sake, your puppy needs to sit on command and come when you call him. Your puppy must know right off the bat which toys he is allowed to chew and which ones — say, your shoes — he isn't. You must express yourself clearly so that your puppy understands which behaviors you desire from him (and which you don't). Your puppy will want to please you, but he won't know how unless you tell him.

Another thing you need is a willingness to make this raising and training diary your new companion. Take it with you when you walk your puppy, or when you and he go for a ride in the car. Take it with you when your puppy goes in for his veterinary checkups, or when you visit the park. As soon as you're done with a quick training session, record what you did and how it went. If you write things down right away, it's fun and easy. If you wait until later, it becomes a chore.

Knowing how busy you are, this diary won't assume you're able to train your puppy every single day. In the diary section, you can customize pages for when you *are* training your puppy. And because puppies are living, breathing creatures with personalities of their own, some days you'll want to write down every single adorable thing about your puppy; other days you won't!

How This Book Is Organized

The book is divided into parts, each with its own colorful theme. In the opening chapter you'll find out more about how this book is organized and receive some important general, puppy care advice.

After that, you'll arrive at the central focus of this book: the raising and training diary. This part allows you to customize a puppy raising and training plan according to your puppy's needs, your own goals, and your personal schedule. You'll also have a place to record each session and monitor your puppy's progress. Each spread is complete with a puppy care and training fact that will pique your interest in your new pet.

Icons Used in This Book

The icons in this book point out various things to you:

 Useful tidbits and helpful advice — like how to rescue your favorite shoe from your puppy's mouth — without his thinking that you're playing a game.

 "Warning, Warning!" You should definitely pay attention here! Need I say more?

 Friendly reminders to help your puppy flourish — like leaving him a full bowl of water on a hot summer day.

Where to Go from Here

Getting started today is the most important step in puppy training. Before you know it, your puppy will be a dog. The sooner you begin to make use of this book, the sooner you can start your puppy on the track to good behavior and fine manners.

Part I

I've Picked Out My Pup — What's Next?

The 5th Wave · By Rich Tennant

Beware of Dog

THUNDER

"We're hoping he'll grow into it."

In this part...

Congratulations. You've selected the perfect puppy for you. Feelings of pride, adoration, and love are emanating all around you.

Out of nowhere, the dreaded "What should I do now?" thought pops into your head. Well, don't hold your breath another minute. In this part, you learn what to buy, what to do after you bring your puppy home, how to understand your new friend, and how to think like a dog.

You also get the scoop on basic training lessons — from teaching your puppy some control and manners to teaching your puppy basic commands.

Chapter 1

Creating a Comfortable Home for Your Puppy

*Y*ou need to make some preparations before the Big Day arrives — when you actually bring home your new puppy. You must get supplies to outfit your home: upfront essentials like a good collar, a few leashes, a realistic containment system, and a few odds and ends. This chapter walks you through the stuff you need.

Soon after you bring home your puppy, you need to start working on another set of supplies — training supplies. This chapter also fills you in on the essentials for getting your puppy's training started. And because you need to consider outdoor enclosures too, this chapter gives you a few options to think about.

Outfitting Your Home with Necessities

The day has arrived — time to pull out your plastic and do a little shopping for your new family member. Although you may be tempted to buy every gimmick — from the latest toy to that designer doggy raincoat — I suggest that you bring a list and stick to it. The more important items are discussed in this section.

You need to designate an area where your mischievous puppy stays while you're not home and where he cools off when things get out of hand. I like to think of this area as a cubby because it needs to be small, quiet, and cozy. Don't worry, it reminds them of their wolfish den roots. You can create a cubby by gating your puppy into a small area or buying a crate or playpen for him.

Puppy-proofing with gates

Gates are a big help in raising a puppy. You can use them to cubby your puppy in a small area, such as a bathroom or enclose a play area. Kitchens make an ideal play area because they don't isolate your puppy from you.

If you use a gate to create your puppy's cubby, make sure that you pick an area that has linoleum or tile floors, which are easier to clean in case of accidents. You also want to ensure that the area is puppy-proofed.

Containing cutie in a crate

Crates are comforting for puppies who don't know how to handle open spaces. They also are useful for toilet training. Crates are good in the following situations:

- When your puppy must be left unattended for less than six hours
- During sleeping hours for young, unhousetrained, or mischievous puppies
- As a time-out area for overexcitable pups

You can choose from several different types of crates, but they come in two general varieties. Portable travel kennels are made from polypropylene. Wire or mesh crates, some of which fold down nicely, are sturdier and provide better ventilation — definitely a must in hot environments. Both do the job.

Following are a few things to keep in mind about crates:

- ✔ The size of the crate is important, especially if you're housetraining a puppy.

- ✔ If the crate is too large, the puppy may eliminate in one end and sleep in the other.

Crates are a valuable training tool, but they also can be emotionally destructive to your puppy if overused. Too many people expect their pups to be able to stay crated all day long and still be good dogs.

If your puppy still has a lot of growing to do, and you don't want to have to buy a puppy crate now and an adult-sized crate later, buy an adult-sized crate with a crate divider. Divide it so that your puppy can only lie comfortably and turn around. Do the same if you have a big dog and a bigger crate. If no manufactured dividers are available, create one out of a safe, nontoxic material.

Dogs love to pee on absorbent surfaces. If you're still having house training problems, consider the bedding you're using. Is it thick and plush? If so, maybe it's too plush — change it if needed.

If you can, place the crate in a bedroom because puppies and dogs hate being alone at night. If having the crate in the bedroom is out of the question, place it in a well-trafficked room, like the kitchen or family room.

Do not use the crate if you're gone for long eight- to 12-hour days. Being confined in a relatively small space for such a long period of time will drive your dog nuts. Isolated all day in a kennel, he'll learn to sleep during the day and keep you up all night. You'll create a nocturnal nightmare with the energy of six stallions, which isn't good for either of you.

Providing extra room in a canine playpen

Do you work all day? In addition to hiring a dog walker, consider purchasing a canine playpen (often called X pens). Playpens enclose your puppy, preventing destruction and at the same time giving him plenty of room to stretch and move about. You can open the playpen during work hours and fold it down when you're at home.

Leading with good leashes

You'll discover more about leashes in the age-appropriate pages of your puppy diary. For now, all you need to purchase is a lightweight nylon leash and a long line, which you use for outdoor playtime in open areas (away from streets) and, later, for advanced training.

Slipping on a regular tag collar

Have a buckle collar and tag waiting for your new arrival (see Figure 1-1 for collar options). If you're getting a puppy, purchase a lightweight nylon collar and a small tag. (Don't worry if you haven't picked out a name; a good tag needs to give your phone number with a short message, such as a "Help Me Get Home 666-555-4444.") When fit properly, you should be able to comfortably slip two fingers under the collar. Check the fit often if you have a puppy — they grow faster than you'd think.

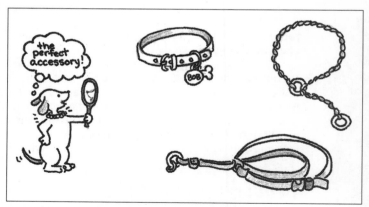

Figure 1-1: Various training collars are available.

Home, Home at Last

You made it home with your puppy, somehow. You've been anxiously waiting for this moment. The excitement level is probably pretty high, so take a few deep breaths. Too much tension can startle or frighten a young puppy. Even though you want to rush in and give your newest member the full tour, hold your huskies.

Pick one room ahead of time, clean it, decorate it with bowls and bedding, and take your new pup or dog there first. Share his curiosity as he checks out the room. Speak to him sweetly. If your dog has an accident or grabs something inappropriate, don't correct him. He's too disoriented to retain anything so soon, and you'll just frighten him. So relax. This is just the beginning.

Keep the kids calm

Talk about excitement. The day you first bring your puppy home may be on the future "fondest memories of my childhood" list. However, your job is to keep the kids calm. Too much squealing and loving in the first five minutes can be overwhelming for a pup. Explain the situation to your kids ahead of time and ask for their help in making the dog or puppy feel comfortable.

Set limits. Make a rule that children can follow the puppy quietly and speak gently, but all roughhousing, shouting, and fighting are forbidden. (This may be your last peaceful moment for a while, so enjoy it.)

Make harmony with your other pets

Having patience when introducing your new puppy to your other pets is important. Keep in mind that animals are territorial and protective of their environment. But if you follow a few simple guidelines, the whole gang should get along fine. Eventually.

Other/older dogs

Older dogs don't like sharing their space with puppies. So make the first introductions on neutral ground before bringing them together in your home.

You'll probably see a lot of bluffing — showing of the teeth, raised hackles, and shoulder pawing — when the two first meet. It all looks pretty scary but rarely escalates to a fight, so stay calm and don't interfere. (Don't interfere, that is, unless you see an unusually aggressive response — glaring eyes, withdrawn lips, and a growl that starts in the throat or belly.) Here are some other harmless behaviors you may see:

- ✔ Some older dogs will growl or paw at a new puppy — this is a good sign. Big dog is showing little dog who's boss.

- ✔ Sometimes new dogs shriek if the resident dog even comes near; again, don't interfere. If you comfort the new dog, it may alienate your resident dog and make the relationship between them rocky.

To keep the hierarchy harmonious, pay more attention to your resident dog, greeting and feeding her first. As long as she feels like she's still number one in your heart, she should cope just fine. Although you may find it hard not to meddle and feel protective of your newcomer, remember, you're following dog pack rules.

Cats

Cats have mixed feelings about new dogs. Some cats head for the highest object in the house and stare at you reproachfully. Some wait confidently for the curious dog to get close enough for a good solid bat on the nose. In either case, keep your response low-key. Overreacting makes both animals nervous.

If your cat can't come to grips with the presence of the new puppy, keep the two in separate areas and bring them together when your dog has undergone more obedience training.

Small animals

If you have other caged animals in the house, like ferrets or guinea pigs, don't bring them out immediately. Let the puppy get used to you and then show him the cages when he's in a sleepy mood.

How the first 24 hours will go

The first day that your new puppy is at home with you can be a little odd. After all the anticipation and preparation, your puppy has arrived. Some puppies jump right into the swing of things; others prefer a more reserved approach. Don't compare your puppy to others you've known and don't worry if he seems too rambunctious, too cautious, or too anything. You, your house, and the other people and pets there are new to him; he's trying to figure out what's going on.

If your puppy wants to sleep, let him sleep. Put him in his crate (or sleep area) with the door open. At mealtime, put his food and water bowl in or near his crate and leave him alone for 15 minutes. Even if he doesn't touch his food, take it up. (It's probably just his nerves.) After the meal, walk him outside or to the newspapers. Water needs to be made available during meal times and removed with the food. Leave a dish by the door, allowing sips before each outing, and be mindful that if your puppy looks thirsty, he probably is.

Ideally, your dog needs to sleep near you at night, by your bedside in a large open-topped box or crate that he can't climb out of. He may whine the first few nights, but he'll feel a lot safer beside your bed than alone in another room. If he whines, lay your hand in the box or on the crate to calm him.

What to Expect the First Week

Having a puppy is a big change, and the first week's a whirlwind. You wake up and remind yourself that you have an extra mouth to feed (unless, of course, that extra mouth is yelping at you for some attention). Even though it's only human to envision every piddle as a lifelong habit, try not to feel overwhelmed. The more important things are taking care of your puppy's need to eat, sleep, play, piddle, and poop. Just like a newborn.

Chapter 2

Early Training for You & Your Puppy

· ·

In This Chapter

▶ Being a good puppy trainer

▶ Training yourself first

▶ Recognizing your puppy's unique personality

▶ Remedying daily hassles

▶ Quickly solving your puppy's behavior woes

▶ Motivating your puppy to work with you

· ·

*B*eing able to talk to animals was my lofty aspiration at the age of 2. In reality, although they may not actually "talk" to them, plenty of people have a way with animals. You can recognize them in a heartbeat. They can walk into your house and have your puppy behaving in seconds and looking to them as their long-lost leader. When I did this with one particular 8-month-old puppy, it was enough to bring one of my clients (the dog's owner) to tears. "Why doesn't Alice look at me that way?" she asked.

Alice eventually did look at her owner that way, but first I taught the owner what I knew by instinct and experience — a new thought pattern that began with respect for her pup and an understanding of how she, the owner, had played a role in creating the problem with her dog. In this chapter, I share with you what I shared with her. I help you become a good dog trainer before you begin working with your dog. The stuff in this chapter can help you better understand and train your dog.

You Gotta Train Yourself First

A great deal goes into being a good dog trainer, and most of it's a mental thing. Puppies have spirits, just like the rest of us, that you must understand and encourage in ways that make sense to your dog. Your puppy has bestowed on you the highest honor, one you'd never receive from a human: a lifetime commitment to respect your judgment and abide by your rules. You need only to show her how.

To show your puppy how, you need to remember the key things that a good dog trainer does:

- ✔ Accepts and modifies his own personality
- ✔ Never blames the pup
- ✔ Recognizes the pup's unique personality
- ✔ Understands his (the trainer's) role in the training process

Recognizing and Modifying Your Personality

Now's the time to analyze yourself. Take out a pen and paper and write down three adjectives to describe your personality. What kind of person are you? Demanding? Sweet? Forgiving? Compulsive? Be honest!

Are you demanding, but your dog is a sweetie? If so, someone is going to have to change. Making too many demands on a sweet dog only frightens her; she'll shut down or run away when training begins. If you're compulsive and you have a laid-back dog, you'll be laughed at. Have you ever seen a dog laugh at his owner? It's quite embarrassing.

For you to be a good dog trainer, you must modify your personality to suit your dog's.

Never Blame the Pup

Believe it or not, puppies don't act out of spite. Your puppy's behavior is directly related to your reactions. My mantra?

A dog repeats whatever gets attention.

Whatever gets attention. And they don't care whether the attention is negative or positive. So if you're out there saying, "I tell her she's bad, but she just ignores me!" I have something to tell you: Your dog interprets your discipline as interaction, and so she'll repeat the unwanted behavior again and again.

So how do you handle unruly situations? The first step to becoming a good dog trainer is to stop blaming the dog.

Recognize the Pup's Unique Personality

Yes, puppies have personalities, too. If you've had more than one, I'm sure you know exactly what I'm talking about. So many of my clients have started their sob stories with "My last dog was so easy!" "But," I respond with a smile, "this isn't your last dog. This dog is unique (see Figure 2-1). And to train her, you must begin by understanding her personality."

Figure 2-1: Recognize your pup's unique personality.

The six common character types

Based on my experience through the years working with countless numbers of dogs, I've noticed that most dogs fit into one of six character types. Identify your puppy's character type and remember it as you work through the training chapters later in this book.

Eager Beaver

These creatures do whatever is required to make you happy, but they can be difficult and manic if you ignore their training. Eager Beavers want to please so much that they stick to whatever gets attention. If you like to toss the ball, puppies with this personality will bring it back 500 times. If you encourage jumping, these dogs will jump on you — and everyone else — whenever excitement builds. If you encourage them to sit and settle down on command, that's what they'll do. With this puppy, all you have to do is decide what you want. You don't need to use harsh training techniques.

Joe Cool

Laid back and relaxed, a puppy with this personality has control of every situation and seems to be less focused on you than her image. Give these puppies a command, and they'll look at you as if to say, "in a minute," and then they'll forget. Organize a lesson, and they'll fall asleep. Although they're quite funny and easy to live with, training is essential for these dogs. Without it, they may not respond to you off lead. They may also be unmanageable in social situations. Diligent and patient training techniques are necessary.

The Jokester

I've owned a little comedian. A quick-minded perfectionist. Calvin taught me more about dog training than a lot of books I've read. The reason? Dogs with this personality are revved up Wonder Pups who get into plenty of trouble it they're not directed. Dancing on the edge of good behavior, they're biggest accolade is laughter, and they must be firmly persuaded to cooperate. Laughter, after all, is attention — trust me, it's hard not to laugh at a dog prancing around with an oversized cantaloupe in her mouth. Given clear, consistent, and stern instruction, comedians take to training well. Their puppyhood will test your patience, but they make wonderful dogs if trained.

The Bully

These dogs take themselves far too seriously. In a pack of puppies, this pup would've been destined to lead, and your home is no different. Unless you're experienced, a pup of this nature can be difficult to train. Aggression, physical leaning, and mounting are common. Training must be consistent and firm and needs to begin in puppyhood. If your dog fits this profile, you must lay down the law now, and you may need professional training. Do not proceed with training on your own if your puppy threatens you.

Sweetie Pie

Docile and mild, these puppies like to observe situations rather than control them. They adore the people they love and must be trained under a soft hand. If you yell at them — or at anyone else — they crumble. There's little to say against these dear puppies. Although it's easy to skip over training for these pups, training is essential for their safety.

Scaredy Cat

These puppies like to view the world from behind your legs. Soothe this behavior, and you make it worse. Unlike children, who may feel relieved, soothing actually reinforces the dog's fear. You must act confident and relaxed in new and startling situations. Tell your puppy "excuse me," and move her away if she ducks behind you. Only reinforce her if she calms down. Training is essential to help these characters feel more secure. These puppies respond best to a gentle hand.

Psychotic pups are out there

It's rare that I come across a psychotic puppy, but they do exist. Some puppies have been bred poorly and suffer brain damage as a result. These dogs can become vicious and are a danger even as young puppies. This problem is identified by erratic or fearful aggression responses in atypical situations. There are two categories:

> ✔ **Erratic viciousness.** At unpredictable intervals, puppies with erratic viciousness growl fiercely from the belly. It may happen when her owner passes her food bowl, approaches when she's chewing a toy, or even walks by her. At other times, the puppy is perfectly sweet — a "Jekyll and Hyde" personality.

✔ **Fear biters.** These puppies show dramatic fear in or a startled bite response to nonthreatening situations, like turning a page of the newspaper or moving an arm. They can act extremely confused or threatened when strangers approach.

Many well-educated dog people use the term fear biter incorrectly. A big difference exists between a dog that bites out of fear and a fear biter. Don't automatically assume the worst if someone labels your dog with this term.

Dealing with aggression

Don't panic if your puppy occasionally growls at you in play or barks at the mailman. A lot of puppies growl when protecting a food dish or toy, and the guarding instinct is strong in many breeds. These are behavioral problems that can be cured or controlled with proper training. Even many biters can be rehabilitated.

A dog may bite for many different reasons. Aggression can be related to a dog's need for dominance, her desire to guard an object, a person, or a place, or it can be simple, old-fashioned fear.

Dominance

If you have a dominant pup under your roof — one who steals clothing for fun, barks for attention, leans against you in new environments or around strangers, you need to regain control of your puppy now, before she grows up into a mean dog, by:

✔ Ignoring all your pup's attempts to get your attention, including but not limited to barking, pawing, headbutting, and whining.

✔ Avoiding stare downs unless you initiate them, in which case make sure your pup breaks eye contact first.

✔ Regulating feeding to twice a day. Don't give food rewards or treats until your aggression problems are history.

Spatial aggression (object guarding)

A dog who shows aggression while eating, sleeping, grooming, or being medicated by a family member, stranger, or other dog professional is showing spatial aggression.

If you see this behavior, don't freak out, hit your puppy, or scream. These reactions only reinforce his defensive notion that you've come to steal his prize. To help your pup accept you as less threatening, follow these steps:

- Don't make a power struggle out of the feeding ritual.

- Shake a plastic cup with some small dog biscuits and reward your puppy with one. Keep doing this until your puppy connects the sound with a reward.

- Approach your puppy once a day with the treat cup while she's eating a meal. If she growls as you approach her during a meal, stop and toss her a few treats before you leave.

- Repeat the previous steps until you can stand over your puppy and drop treats into her bowl.

Territorial aggression

Dogs who act aggressively when strangers approach their homes are territorial. The following encourages this problem:

- When delivery people approach, enter, and then leave the home territory, your puppy thinks that she's driven them away. Her aggression is reinforced.

- When the owners are home and react to a dog's territorial response by yelling at or physical handling her, the dog perceives their heightened response as backup, a job well done.

To prevent further territorial aggression, assert yourself by keeping your puppy off all furniture. Putting her through a regimented training program should help. Try the following:

- Make associations with visitors more positive by using a treat cup or peanut butter jar to help your puppy associate outsiders with a positive, yummy reward.

  Peanut butter jar — how's that? Yes, dogs love peanut butter. Get them their own little jar and tape a bell to it to help them associate peanut butter with a special sound. When visitors arrive, have them offer the jar to your puppy *after* she's settled down.

- Eliminate all yelling and physical corrections. They add more negative energy to an already tense situation.

Protective aggression

Does your puppy feel responsible for you? Even outside of her territory, does she react aggressively if anyone approaches? If your pup's acting like your guard wherever you go, you have a serious identity crisis to deal with. She thinks it's her job to protect you. You must let your puppy know that you're the boss by:

- Keeping your pup behind you at all thresholds — including doors and stores, even at the veterinarian's office.

- Making sure that when you meet new people your pup isn't standing in front of you. You, not your dog, should always be first to greet visitors.

Predatory aggression

Predatory aggression is another instinctive behavior from times when dogs were wolves and hunted for their survival. Most dogs still possess the chasing instinct. Although we have suppressed the drive to kill in most breeds, some — Nordic breeds and Terriers especially — instinctively chase (and occasionally kill) small game. Your hands are full if you have a chaser. That kind of pup needs a focused activity to keep her busy. Try

- Involving her in games on a routine basis. Check out Chapter 6 for interactive games that will appeal to her predatory instincts. The two of you are sure to get a great workout.

- Making sure you're present in the company of small children and other, smaller animals so that you can discourage the chasing ritual. When your pup gets ready to stalk, distract her with a toy or a treat cup.

Fear-induced aggression

Every litter has its shy puppies — mama's boys or girls who depend on her wisdom for safety. In human homes, these dogs continue to be needy. Their timidity, which surfaces in new situations, may turn into overwhelming fear.

Although shyness is a temperamental trait, this behavior has a learned element: Soothing a frightened puppy doesn't alleviate her fear; it reinforces it. To help prevent fear-induced aggression, you must assert yourself as the one who's calm, in control, and in charge of the situation. Here are some extra tips:

- ✔ Keep your puppy on a leash when you expect company. Hold her leash and act confidently when the two of you venture into new surroundings.

- ✔ Encourage everyone to ignore your puppy until *she* approaches them.

- ✔ Use a treat cup or peanut butter jar to encourage better behavior in a new or tricky situation.

- ✔ If you decide to seek professional help for your shy pup, find a trainer who uses a soft, positive approach. Threatening this type of dog only creates more fear.

Training to Remedy Daily Hassles

What you consider bad behavior can be extremely frustrating. After all, no one likes having chewed carpets, scratched doors, or company that hides from a jumping puppy when you open the door. The first step in resolving actions you don't approve of is to understand that you and your puppy don't share the same worldview. When your puppy jumps on company, he's enjoying every minute of the chaos that follows. A chewed carpet usually is a sign of boredom, anxiety, or teething. To resolve the behaviors that you don't like, you have to look at them from your puppy's perspective and then modify your behavior to change his reactions.

The process isn't too difficult, but you need a few guidelines to get on the right track. In this chapter, I cover jumping, barking, chewing, the infamous grab-and-go, and *nipping*. Nipping is a puppy thing; it's interactive and playful. Nipping puppies are bossy and manipulative. They need a firmer regimen. By following my advice in this chapter, you'll soon earn the reward of seeing a change in your puppy's reaction and behavior.

Grounding the Joyous Jumper

Everybody knows a jumper — a knock-you-over-when-you-come-in jumper, a muddy-paws-on-the-couch jumper, and a counter cruiser (the puppy who likes to sniff along counter-tops). Jumping is a sure-fire attention-getter. So what gives? The first step in solving your problem is to understand how it became a problem in the first place. Once again, your puppy isn't to blame.

Puppies see us as other dogs, and eye contact is a big method of canine communication. Our eyes are above theirs, so to be gracious and greet us properly, puppies must jump. The first time this happens, a hug follows. "Isn't that cute?" After about the tenth jump, it isn't so cute. So the puppy usually gets a shove. But what's a shove to a dog? Confrontational play. The puppy jumps higher and harder the next time. So you try a little toe stepping, paw grabbing, and yelling — all with the same effect. Your dog thinks jumping is interactive and fun.

Counter jumping is another favorite pastime. After all, we're looking at the counter constantly, so why shouldn't the puppy as well? When a dog jumps up, you react by shouting and shoving. The puppy interpretation? *Prize Envy.* The dog thinks, "Whatever I was reaching for must be excellent because everybody raced over for it." So the puppy reconsiders. She jumps when your back is turned or you're out of the room. This behavior isn't spiteful; it's just plain smart. This section helps you dissect and correct the jumping problem one situation at a time.

Dogs that jump need to learn the *Four-Paw Rule* — no attention until all four paws are on the floor.

The best way to remedy jumping when you arrive home is to ignore your pup (see Figure 2-2). Try it for a week.

- ✔ Come home and ignore your dog until she's given up the jumping vigil.

- ✔ Keep a basket of balls or squeaky toys by the door. When you come in, toss one on the ground to refocus your dog's energy.

- ✔ If your dog's crated, don't let her out immediately. Wait until she's calm.

Figure 2-2: Ignore your joyously jumping pup.

Quieting That Bark-Bark-Barker

A barking dog's a real headache — a complete nightmare. How you handle the situation depends on what's prompting the barking in the first place. In the meantime, you need to watch your reaction. The cardinal sin when rehabilitating your barker is for you to yell. When you yell, your dog thinks you're barking, which leads to — you guessed it — more barking — a bark-along. To solve your problem, stay cool.

Barking at e-v-e-r-y-thing

Does your dog bark at everything she sees and hears? Nothing goes unnoticed — a biker, the neighborhood kids, or little lively creatures passing through your yard. For some people, after a while, the dog's barking can seem as much a part of their daily routine as the wind passing through the trees. For those of us who don't fall into that category, however, perpetual barking is a big pain.

Barking has an added lure. Whenever your dog barks at something, whether from the window or the yard, that thing goes away. Sure, you and I know that the postman's going to keep moving, but don't tell your dog. She thinks her strength and prowess drove the postman away — quite an ego boost.

So how do you organize your team and teach your dog the rules? You have to understand what motivates your dog's behavior and you have to master her communication skills.

All this may seem like hard work, but watching the technique in action is quite fascinating. Your dog will respond to you more willingly if you make the effort to understand and learn her language. With an ounce of effort, a little time, and some structure, you can earn your dog's respect, cooperation, and trust. Plus, you'll have a teammate who will be at your side when the cards are down. You can't beat that bargain!

Start training immediately. Dogs who bark at everything perceive themselves (not you) as the leader, and one of the leader's duties is to guard her territory and her group from intruders. Your dog needs to understand that you're the boss.

Avoid leaving your puppy alone outdoors for long stretches of time. Unsupervised confinement often breeds boredom and territorial behavior. Put those two together, and you're likely to end up with a barkaholic.

Block off areas that your puppy uses as lookout posts such as a living room couch or windowsill. If she's a night guard, secure her on lead in your room at night. Give her 3 feet of freedom — just enough to lie comfortably on her bed.

Screaming at your puppy is translated into barking. Your puppy feels supported, and her role as leader (she barked first) is reinforced. Anytime you see (or hear) your dog start to perk up, say "Shh" and call her to your side. If she ignores you, place her on the teaching lead or let her drag a leash so you can quickly gain control.

Many collars are on the market to help discourage the barking habit. Although I've never tried the electrical stimulation collars (my dog would freak out), I've used the citronella collars, which spray citronella toward the muzzle if barking is continuous.

Barking in the car

Being locked in a car with a barking dog is my version of purgatory. The car creates an effect similar to the territorial situation described in the preceding section. Your dog barks, and the passing object disappears — only faster in the case of a moving car.

Yelling at your dog isn't the thing to do. Pleading doesn't win you any brownie points. This problem tends to disappear slowly as you progress through training; however, you can do a few things in the interim to discourage this behavior:

✔ Enforce stillness while you drive. Station your puppy in the car with a seat belt safety lead.

✔ Have your puppy pause before you let her enter or exit the car. Instruct "Wait" and give her permission to enter with "OK." After all, the car is yours, not hers.

✔ Play classical music and stay cool. Your dog perceives any frustration on your part as backup and ups the ferocity.

✔ If your situation is unbearable, secure your dog on a chin lead.

✔ Ignore the barking if your car's moving. Driving is a job in itself.

✔ If you're stationary, try to spritz your dog lightly with a plant mister (without turning and glaring).

✔ If your dog barks at gas-station or toll-booth attendants, ask them to toss a piece of cheese into the car window from afar. The hope is that your dog will make a more positive association (see Chapter 5 for more about safely taking your puppy with you in the car).

Barking for attention or protest

All puppies go through a phase when they can't bear to be left alone. If you soothe a protest or attention barker, you end up with a real spoiled dog on your hands. If you ignore the situation, your partner may threaten to leave you. Is there a happy medium? Well, not really, but I'll give it my best shot:

- Ignore the barking if you can. Never yell.

- Avoid grandiose departures and arrivals. They're too exciting.

- Place peanut butter in a hollow bone and give it to your dog as you leave.

- Return to your puppy only after she's calmed down. If you must interfere with a barking tantrum, go to her quietly without eye contact or comments.

Stopping the Chewing Frenzy

Chewing is a puppy thing. It's nothing personal. They don't know a stick from a table leg or a doll's head from a chestnut. Fortunately, they can be rehabilitated. If you have a chewer on your hands, be patient and use some of the tried-and-true techniques described next.

Getting bitter apple . . . and lots of it

Bitter apple is nasty tasting stuff that you can buy at most pet stores. You spray it on things you want to prevent your dog from chewing. If you notice your puppy chewing on the furniture surrounding her station, spray everything but her bed and bone. Never spray bitter apple on your puppy — it's for objects only.

Believe it or not, some puppies actually like bitter apple. If your pup is one of these, try some red pepper juice with a little garlic or Tabasco sauce.

Being aware of prize envy

If you yell at your dog after she's begun to grab an object that she shouldn't or after she's finished chewing, you only damage your relationship with her. Yelling afterward communicates Prize Envy — what's being grabbed is valuable because of the challenge of getting it back. If you give the correction too late, your dog thinks, "Wow, what a great prize. Everybody wants to take it from me!" Instead of disciplining after the fact, set up situations so that you can correct your puppy's *grab-and-go* thought process. Discovering the value of treat cups after the dog has already gotten ahold of something you don't want her to have will help.

Kissing it good-bye

If your puppy destroys something, let it go. Yelling or hitting your puppy only makes her nervous and frightened, which leads to more chewing. Any puppy owner can commiserate, and I know firsthand how angry you feel, but don't take your anger out on your pup. She doesn't know any better. Remember, your puppy's mouth is equivalent to your hands; if your dog is nervous or fidgety, she chews. I'm sure if your dog could surf the Net, scan the soaps, or pull her hair out, she would, but since she can't, chewing has to do.

Dogs do things that are natural to them: eat food, pick up objects (with their teeth, of course), and investigate trash bins. Instead of losing your cool, which only frightens your dog, try the options mentioned in this book. You and your dog will be glad you did.

Offering one main toy plus a surplus of surprises

Having too many objects to choose from can confuse your dog. Pick a bone or toy that satisfies your puppy's penchant for chewing, buy multiples of that item, and spread them around the house for quick and easy access. Here are some other suggestions:

> ✔ Keep your supply of play toys in a special place (designating a box or drawer), bringing them out for special interaction times.
>
> ✔ Designate one toy that's only offered during greetings. I use a hollow bone stuffed with peanut butter.

Your Role in the Training Process

One of my clients called me in jubilation one day. After weeks of group training, she had figured it out. "Training is about getting the puppies to want to work with you!"

In class, I repeat the same concept many different ways. However, I understand that hearing the words and feeling their meaning rarely happen simultaneously. Although this student had listened to me, she had been training her dog by dictating her commands and muscling through all corrections. Additionally, she carried out my suggestions to the extreme: If I said to enunciate commands, she'd shout them. When I encouraged people to tap their foot lightly to end a heel, she'd stamp it.

She loves her dog tremendously, but when she started training, she was more obsessed with the mechanics than the process itself. "Remember," I would tell her, "training involves two spirits — yours and your puppy's. One affects the other." To understand your role in the training process, keep these things in mind:

> ✔ Training is about making your puppy want to work with you.
>
> ✔ Your puppy isn't a machine; he's a spiritual being.
>
> ✔ Every puppy learns at a different rate.
>
> ✔ Frustration is catching, so stay calm.
>
> ✔ Your mom's right — patience is a virtue.

Chapter 3

Communicating with Your Puppy

Communicating with your puppy involves more than just talking to him. Dogs learn to interpret your behavior by the way you move (body language), by the tone of your voice, and by the way you look at them.

Talking to Your Puppy

Keep in mind that puppyhood is the best time to make a good impression on your dog. Because sudden moves may startle him, try to tread lightly around your new pet, especially at first.

Body language

Body language is important to puppies. Remember, English isn't puppy's first language. Puppies learn by observation from one another, from their mothers, and from you. Keep that in mind *before* raising your voice. Puppies are extremely intuitive at reading your body language.

Stand upright and relax when directing your dog. I call this the *peacock position*. When giving your puppy direction or a command, throw your shoulders back and stand tall just like a peacock.

Tone

Did you immediately start talking baby talk to your new puppy? If so, you're on the right track. But baby talk isn't the best way to get your puppy to follow your directions. You will need to change your tone to fit the various situations you (and your puppy) find yourself in.

If your puppy thinks of you as another dog and you start yelling, he hears barking. Barking (yelling) interrupts behavior; it doesn't instruct. And barking increases excitement. Yelling is just no good! It is far better to concentrate on using the appropriate tone when speaking to your dog. These three tones work wonders.

Delighted tone

Use this tone when you want to praise your puppy (see Figure 3-1). It needs to be soothing to him. It isn't intended to excite him. Find a tone that makes your pup feel warm and proud inside.

Teaching kids how to use the proper tone

If you have kids, you've probably noticed that sometimes they call out to puppies in a high-pitched tone, and sometimes they don't pronounce commands properly. And you're probably wondering what to do about it.

Well, until kids are 12, you're better off focusing on what they're doing right rather than honing in on their imperfections. So my advice is simply to overenunciate all your commands so that the kids find out how to pronounce them properly in an appropriate tone. For example, rather than saying "Sit, " stretch it out by saying *"Siiit."* If you overenunciate each command, your kids notice the effects and start mimicking you. And when your kids copy your intonations, the control transfers from you to them.

Figure 3-1: Communicate your delight by your tone of voice.

Directive tone

Use this tone for your commands. It must be clear and authoritative, not harsh or sweet. Give your commands while standing in the peacock position.

Discipline tone

I'm not much of a disciplinarian. My approach encourages more structure than strictness, but you need to have a few tones that tell your dog to back off or move on. The tone shouldn't be shameful or disapproving, like "How could you?" or "You better not touch that." Discipline has more to do with timing than your puppy's transgressions.

Don't repeat your commands. Dogs don't understand words; they interpret sounds. Saying "Sit, sit, sit, Boomer, sit!" sounds much different than "SIT" — and that's what Boomer learns. If you want your dog to listen when you give the first command, make sure you give it only once; then reinforce your expectations by positioning your dog.

Who's In Charge Here, Anyway?" (Communicating Leadership)

Dogs have plenty of team spirit. Many often refer to this as their "pack instinct," but I like to think of it in "team" terms. Team consciousness and the canine psyche have a great deal in common. Teams focus on winning; each player works for it, wants it, thinks about it, and strives for it. Dogs live their entire lives, their every waking moment, by team structure. Instead of winning, however, their mantra is survival. And to your dog, you and your family are his team.

Some other, less obvious factors also determine a team's success. Three that come to mind immediately are cooperation, structure, and mutual respect. Without these, even a group of phenomenal players produces only chaos. A good team is organized so that all members know who's in charge and what's expected from them. And if someone gets in trouble or gets hurt, he can trust that another teammate will help.

For your dog to feel secure and safe, he *must* know who's in charge, and teaching him what you expect is your job. In dog land, teams are organized in a hierarchy, so you must teach your four-legged friend that two-legged dogs are the ones in charge. If you have more than one person in your household, teaching this concept requires some cooperation on everyone's part, but it's doable.

Why negative attention doesn't work

Picture an excited jumping puppy. You're trying to read the paper calmly, but he wants your attention. What if you tried to correct the dog by pushing him down and screaming "Off!"? In all likelihood, the puppy will jump again. Do you know why? Because you just gave him attention. Attention in a dog's mind includes anything from dramatic body contact to a simple glance. Yes, even looking at your dog reinforces his behavior.

Though this phenomenon may sound far-fetched at first, it's actually pretty elementary. Puppies think of us as other dogs. If they get excited and then we get excited, we're following their lead. The fact that you may be upset with their behavior just doesn't register. Being upset is a human emotion. Excitement and body contact are dog things. Even if you push your puppy so hard that he stops and slinks away, the only thing you've accomplished is scaring him. And who wants to train a dog through fear? Trust me, there is a better way.

Let me give you another example. What happens if a dog grabs a sock and everyone in the household stops to chase him? Dog party? You bet. Because the puppy views everybody as a dog, he's thinking, "What fun!" as he dives behind the couch and under the table. Chasing doesn't come across as discipline; it comes across as *Prize Envy* — "Whatever I have must be really good because everyone wants it!"

If you don't organize the team hierarchy, your *dog* will, and that can be a real nightmare. If your dog has the personality to lead, you'll find yourself living in an expensive doghouse under dog rule. If your dog doesn't have the personality to lead but feels he must because no one else will, you'll end up with one big headache because dogs in that state are hyper and confused.

The benefits of positive attention

When I ask my clients what they do when they catch their puppy resting or chewing a bone quietly, most say, "Nothing. It's a moment of peace." I appreciate such honesty; however, those are the times when they ought to be showering their puppy with attention. Not wild, twist-and-shout, hoot-and-holler attention. Just calm, soothing, loving attention that makes the puppy smile inside. A soft whispering praise is best mixed with a massage-like pat. My mantra? Your dog will repeat whatever you pay attention to.

Puppies mimic their leader's energy levels. If you come home to an excited dog and you get excited, you're sending the message that his excitement is acceptable. Instead, come in calm and wait until your puppy's settled down before greeting him.

Knowing the Difference Between Praise and Petting

When your puppy behaves well or learns something new, it's exciting for everyone. But try to control yourself. If you get all fired up and communicate excitement, you'll also get your puppy fired up. Learning takes plenty of concentration, and an excited pup can't learn much. As you practice your exercises, remember the difference between praise and petting. Petting comes from your hand; it excites your puppy and communicates play intentions. Praise comes from your voice and eyes and is given from an upright position; it calms your puppy and communicates your leadership.

Chapter 4

House-training

1 wish I had a nickel for every time I hear "She knows it's wrong! Just look at her eyes — guilt's written all over her face." Interestingly enough, although they know you're mad, puppies cannot connect a reaction now to a bathroom thought they had minutes before.

Dogs shouldn't soil the house, but some do, especially young pups. I know — a puddle or poop on the carpet is a wrenching sight, but think about it from the canine perspective. They're puppies, genetically predisposed to cave life, a free-ranging toilet, nature's toys, and an interactive community. They're not human house-proud. Sure, you want your puppy to be respectful of your carpets, but be patient. To be effective, you need to set aside your feelings of frustration and condition habits that jibe with your puppy's instinctive tidiness.

So if toilet training has you down, cheer up. Although teaching your puppy how to behave in your house is no small trick, it's doable — as long as you have the right mind-set. After-the-fact corrections don't help your long-term goal. You need a new approach, outlined start to finish — a program that you can apply whether your target is grass, papers, city cement, or gravel. Pull up a chair. Read this chapter start to finish; then read it again to everyone in the house. When the effort's concentrated, house-training your puppy is just a matter of time.

Getting into a House-training Routine

Believe it or not, your puppy's elimination habits have a pattern. Puppies go after they sleep, after they play, after they eat, and after long bouts of confinement. As you prepare to house-train your puppy, be aware of these habits.

And be patient. You can train some puppies in days; with others, training may take months. The best way to house-train your puppy is to establish a strategy and follow a consistent routine, like this:

- ✔ Use one specific word as you walk your pup to her toilet spot. (See Figure 4-1)
- ✔ The outside toilet area you pick needs to be in a discrete place relatively close to the house.
- ✔ Blaze a trail and be consistent. Always follow the same path to the toilet spot.
- ✔ When you arrive at the toilet spot, ignore your puppy.
- ✔ Don't let your dog roam until she's relieved herself.
- ✔ Don't greet or praise your puppy until after she has pottied.
- ✔ When your puppy's done, greet, praise, and walk her as usual.

Use a command like "Get busy!" as your puppy is eliminating. After a month of saying this phrase while she's in the process of toileting, your puppy learns to go on cue. How cute is that?

Figure 4-1: Establish a routine and use one specific word as you walk your puppy to her toilet spot.

Getting on a Potty-Time Schedule

So just how many potty breaks does your puppy need per day? Well, that depends. Really young puppies — younger than 12 weeks — may need to go outside every hour or two. Older puppies can hold out quite a bit longer. Use the following general guidelines for your puppy:

Puppy's Age	*Number of Potty Breaks a Day*
6 to 14 weeks	**8 to 10**
14 to 20 weeks	**6 to 8**
20 to 30 weeks	**4 to 6**
30 weeks to adult	**3 to 4**

In both Tables 4-1 and 4-2, italicized events may no longer be necessary as your puppy grows up.

Table 4-1	House-training Schedule for Work-at-Home Owners
Time of Day	*Potty Time*
Early morning wake up	Go outside
Breakfast	Go outside after breakfast
Midmorning	*Go outside*
Afternoon feeding	*Go outside after eating*
Mid-afternoon	Go outside
Dinnertime (4 to 6 p.m.)	Go outside after dinner
7:30 p.m.	Remove water
Mid-evening	*Go outside*
Before bed	Go outside
Middle of the night	Go outside if necessary

Table 4-2	House-training Schedule for Owners Who Work Outside the Home
Time of Day	*Potty Time*
Early morning wake up	Go outside
Breakfast	Go outside after breakfast
Lunch break feeding & walk	Go outside
Mid-afternoon	*Young puppies must go out*
Arrival home	Go outside
Dinnertime (4 to 6 p.m.)	Go outside after dinner
7:30 p.m.	Remove water
Before bed	Go outside
Middle of the night	Go outside if necessary

If you work outside the home, take heed!

If you expect your puppy to hold her bladder while you're gone during the day, you'll be disappointed. Puppies lack the bladder muscles necessary to accomplish such a feat. If you have to leave your puppy all day, create a space that allows for a good stretch as well as a place to potty. Although your puppy will be confused if you expect her to go outside when you're home, you have little choice.

Select a be-alone space — a small room, for example — or invest in a puppy playpen, which you can find at most pet stores (make sure the flooring is nonabsorbent). Place your dog's bedding, bowls, and toys in one side of the space; cover the other side of the space with papers or wee-wee pads. (Cover more area than necessary, taping it down if your puppy insists on shredding it.) In most cases, a puppy chooses to eliminate in the absorbent area. That's great. Take your puppy outside when you get home and follow the scheduled routine outlined in Table 4-2. To discourage accidents inside, don't allow access to the be-alone space when you're home.

Changing the Routine

Once you have the routine down pat (give it about a week), interrupt it. Instead of chanting "Outside!" lead your puppy to the door. Wait until she gives you a signal to continue. If her signal is subtly staring at the door, call her back to you and pump her up: "What is it? Outside? Good dog!" Then let her out. Repeat the process in rooms farther and farther from the door or her papers.

Are you having trouble getting your dog to give you a signal? Is your dog just too polite to rock the boat? If you can't get your dog to articulate a signal, try hanging bells from the door. Hang them to the side of the door at your dog's nose level. Each time you pass through the door, slap the bells with your *paw* and say "Outside." Soon your dog will join in the fun.

Using Papers versus Going Outside

You may decide that you're going to paper-train your puppy to a spot inside your home instead of teaching your puppy to go outside. That's fine, but you have to get in the mind-set of using either one or the other. Doing both or paper-training in one season only to switch your priorities to outside only confuses your dog.

Paper-training is a good option if you have a small puppy, you live in an apartment, you're physically challenged, or you're just not the outdoor sort. It also has several similarities to outdoor training:

- ✔ Consistently use the same bathroom spot (inside or out).
- ✔ Use a word or phrase — like "Papers" or "Outside" — when you lead your puppy to the area.
- ✔ After bringing your dog to the area, ignore her until she eliminates.
- ✔ As your puppy's eliminating, use a word or phrase like "Get Busy."
- ✔ Do not use the place as a play or interaction area.

Paper-training has some differences when compared with outdoor training, namely that the papers are within the house. If you're paper-training, keep the papers away from your dog's food and water bowls and sleeping areas. Place the papers in a discrete location, like a corner of the kitchen or bathroom, and make sure they're easily accessible to your puppy, even when you're not home.

City Pups versus Country Pups

House-training a puppy is challenging regardless of the environment, but some key similarities and differences exist between living in a metropolis and the countryside.

Here are the similarities:

- ✔ Dogs must learn to go in one area.

- ✔ Until the process is understood, you must use only the outside for elimination.

- ✔ No matter the location, you must coach your dog until she's got the process down pat. Words help direct behavior.

And here are the differences:

- ✔ City dogs must be curbed (taught to eliminate at the curb). Curbing is tough for leg-lifting males who prefer to mark upright objects. Unfortunately, they don't have a choice. When you train your dog, use the curb close to your home.

- ✔ City dogs have to navigate hallways and escalators before reaching their target. Holding a young puppy until you're outside often helps.

- ✔ Many country or suburban dogs have a large property to choose from, which can be a blessing and a curse. The blessings are obvious; however, as you house-train your dog, you must stay with him. Just plopping a puppy outside by himself often creates more anxiety than cooperation. Your puppy performs best when you're there to influence his actions

Regardless of where you live, picking up after your dogs is a good idea. Stools attract bugs and worms. In the city and many suburbs, cleaning up after your dog is the law. Retail scoopers are available at pet stores, or you can do what I do:

1. **Place your hand in a plastic bag.**

2. **Clasp the mess with your bagged hand.**

3. **Turn the bag inside out.**

4. **Dispose of the bag when you get home.**

Bags are easy to carry on walks as well.

Tips for House-training Success

Though house-training a puppy can be a real challenge, you
can take steps to make it easier on both of you. Consistency
is key. Dramatization of the routine helps make learning this
lesson fun.

Start with a small confinement area.

Puppies are den animals, but the classic den wasn't more
than about 90 square feet. Most young or untrained dogs
won't soil the area right around them, but if they can race
upstairs or into an adjacent room, they're more than happy
to relieve themselves there.

So keep your puppy confined. Crate your puppy when you're
out and at night, if she isn't *stationed.* Stationing your dog
means going into each room you'd like your puppy to behave
in and picking a good area for her to settle into — perhaps a
place near the couch in the television room, but away from the
table in the dining room. Decorate this area with a comfy cush-
ion or a blanket and a favorite chew toy. Doing this helps your
puppy identify her special place, her *station.* After she learns
the rules, you can grant her more freedom, but not now.

Knowing when corrections count

If you catch your puppy in the process of eliminating in the
house, startle her: Clap your hands as you say "Ep, Ep, Ep!"
Jump up and down like an excited chimp. Do whatever you
must to get her to stop. Then direct her to the elimination
area as if nothing happened. When she's done, praise her for
finishing.

Knowing when corrections don't count

You're getting mad at a puppy. As much as you'd like to think
she's human, she isn't, and your frustration just makes you

look foolish. Even though I've heard the idea a thousand times, I'm still not convinced that a "puppy understands the meaning of a correction." Sure, you can frighten a puppy into a fearful posture, but scaring her isn't the point you're trying to make.

If you catch her soiling someplace other than her designated area, you can interrupt the process but lay off all other corrections.

Maintaining a stable diet

Avoid changing dog food brands unless your veterinarian directs you to do so. Puppies don't digest the way humans do. Their stomachs can get upset if you change their diets (see Figure 4-2). Laying off of treats also is a good idea until they're house-trained.

Puppies drink water excessively if they're bored or nervous. If your dog is having peeing problems, monitor his water intake by giving him access to his water bowl only during meal times.

Figure 4-2: Maintain a sensible diet.

Special confinement issues for pet store pups

Pet store pups often have a rough go of the don't-soil-in-your-area concept. After all, they had no choice in that early impressionable time away from Mom. If your pet store puppy is having a problem not soiling in his sleeping area, the crate may not be the best option for house-training because it symbolizes a potty area. At night, a young puppy can sleep at your bedside in a large open-topped box. During the day, keep your puppy with you or confine him in a small room, taking him outside or to the papers every half-hour. Take him to the same area, again and again, following the same routine every single day. If you can get another dog to eliminate in this area, that's all the better because the scent gives your puppy the right idea.

Part II
The Puppy Raising & Training Diary

The 5th Wave   By Rich Tennant

"I don't think teaching the puppy how to help you cheat at cards was the training and bonding experience the Vet had in mind."

In this part...

Are you beginning to think that your puppy is as much work as a child? You're right. Both need training and structure. Both need help containing naughty impulses. Both must be socialized properly. And, well, you may need some help to make it all come together.

Here's the very help you need! This diary enables you to customize your own puppy-raising-and-training plan according to your puppy's needs, your own goals, and your personal schedule. Use it to record each session and monitor your puppy's progress. Months later, you can look back to your beginning sessions and see how much progress you and your puppy have made!

Part II

The Puppy Raising & Training Diary

●　●

*T*his is the section of the book that is mostly yours to fill in with your observations. Sure, we offer suggestions about age-appropriate training and feeding for your puppy. We also provide plenty of tips and hints for you to keep in mind as you raise your puppy.

But remember, the diary is for you to keep track of your particular puppy. And, remember, all puppies are individuals. Your puppy's growth and training abilities will take place at his own rate. So feel free to stretch the limits of this journal. If your puppy is a quick learner, he may be potty-trained before week five. In that case, you can skip some of the house-training material in the journal and head right to the next section. Don't forget to note how puppy responds to each training session, and keep track of puppy's diet and exercise in the blanks provided.

Date _____

Monday

_____
_____
_____
_____

Tuesday

_____
_____
_____
_____

Wednesday

_____
_____
_____
_____

Thursday

_____
_____
_____
_____

Friday

_____
_____
_____
_____

Saturday

You'll want to have the following supplies on hand for your new puppy's arrival:

- ❑ Puppy food
- ❑ Grooming brush
- ❑ Chew toy
- ❑ Sterlized long bone
- ❑ Nail clipper
- ❑ Doggie bed
- ❑ water bowls
- ❑ Collar and leash

Make sure that you have one room completely decorated for your puppy. Fill this room with bowls and bedding. Bring him to this room as soon as you arrive home.

_____

_____

_____

Sunday

Teach your puppy her name. Place some Cheerios in a cup and shake it as you call out her name. Do this at various times of the day. Reward your puppy with a treat.

_____

_____

_____

_____

_____

_____

_____

_____

_____

Tip of the Week

Rub a frozen stick of butter on your palm and let your puppy lick your hands — that way, puppy's first associations of home are friendly and positive.

Date _____

Monday

Tuesday

Wednesday

Thursday

Friday

Saturday

Your dog needs to sleep near you at night, by your bedside in a large open-topped box or crate that he can't climb out of. He may whine the first few nights, but he'll feel a lot safer beside your bed than alone in another room. If he whines, lay your hand in the box or on the crate to calm him.

_____

_____

_____

_____

_____

_____

_____

_____

Sunday

Be prepared to get up one to three times during the night when your dog needs to eliminate. Quietly take him to his spot and then back to his enclosure. For more details on house-training, turn to Chapter 4.

_____

_____

_____

_____

_____

_____

_____

_____

_____

Tip of the Week

If, because of allergies or lack of space, you can't keep your puppy with you in the bedroom at night, crate him or enclose him in a small area, such as a bathroom or kitchen. Bring him his favorite chew toy and blanket. Turn off the lights, turn on some classical music, and be ready to walk him if he cries.

Date _____

Monday

_____
_____
_____
_____

Tuesday

_____
_____
_____
_____

Wednesday

_____
_____
_____
_____

Thursday

_____
_____
_____
_____

Friday

_____
_____
_____
_____

Saturday

All puppies have different nutritional needs. One formula just can't suit everyone. Find out as much as you can about the nutritional needs of your puppy. Talk to your veterinarian, breeder, and educated pet store professional to find the diet that is most suited to your puppy.

_____

_____

_____

_____

_____

_____

_____

Sunday

Here are some other feeding tips that you may find useful:

✔ When your puppy is an infant, you need to feed her three to four times a day, taking her out after each meal to eliminate.

✔ If you have a large-breed puppy (a Great Dane or a Mastiff) your veterinarian may recommend feeding her an adult dog food.

✔ If your puppy's tummy is a little upset during her first few days with you, don't worry. She's just getting used to her new surroundings, her new diet, and her new person — you!

_____

_____

 _____

_____

_____

_____

Tip of the Week

Don't feed your puppy fatty meat such as venison, duck, or pork. And avoid junk food — chips, nuts, crackers, and anything spicy — because these foods will make any dog ill. (**NEVER** give your puppy chocolate; even a small amount of chocolate can be deadly!) Try to keep table scraps to a minimum, as an occasional treat.

Date _____

Monday

Tuesday

Wednesday

Thursday

Friday

Saturday

Believe it or not, puppies' elimination habits have a pattern. They go after they sleep, after they play, after they eat, and after long bouts of confinement. As you house-train your puppy, keep those times in mind. The best way to house-train your puppy is to establish a strategy and follow a consistent routine, like this:

- Blaze a trail and be consistent. Always follow the same path to the toilet spot.

- Use one specific word as you walk your pup to his toilet spot.

- Don't let your dog roam around or go on his walk until he's relieved himself.

- When your puppy is done, praise and walk him as usual.

_____

_____

_____

Sunday

_____

_____

_____

_____

_____

_____

_____

_____

_____

_____

_____

_____

_____

Tip of the Week

If you have a small dog or young puppy, don't carry him to his toilet area. Let him walk so that he can learn how to navigate on his own.

Date _____

Monday
_____
_____
_____
_____

Tuesday
_____
_____
_____
_____

Wednesday
_____
_____
_____
_____

Thursday
_____
_____
_____
_____

Friday
_____
_____
_____
_____

Saturday

Make sure that your puppy has an adequate supply of fresh water to drink. If your dog is panting, it's a good bet that she needs a drink. Dry food also encourages thirst because it contains only 10 percent moisture. That means your dog needs about a quart of water for every pound of dry food that she eats.

_____
_____
_____
_____
_____
_____
_____
_____
_____

Sunday

Put your puppy's collar on her at 20-minute intervals throughout the day until she accepts it.

_____
_____
_____
_____
_____
_____
_____
_____
_____
_____

Tip of the Week

If it's been a month since you last gave your puppy her dose of heartworm medication, now's the time to give her another pill.

Date _____

Monday
_____
_____
_____
_____

Tuesday
_____
_____
_____
_____

Wednesday
_____
_____
_____
_____

Thursday
_____
_____
_____
_____

Friday
_____
_____
_____
_____

Saturday

Regardless of whether your dog has long hair or short, curly, or straight, you need to groom him on a weekly basis. Decide on a grooming day for your pup and set up an area where he's comfortable and where it's easy for you to tend to him.

_____
_____
_____
_____
_____
_____
_____
_____
_____

Sunday

Whether grooming is a chore or a delight is determined in puppyhood. Keep the first brushing episodes fun, ending on a positive note with a treat or favorite toy.

_____
_____
_____
_____
_____
_____
_____
_____
_____

Tip of the Week

Early handling benefits you and your veterinarian. Before your puppy gets ill, make sure he's used to having his paws, ears, belly, and tail manipulated as if you were grooming or medicating him. That way, you won't be confronted with a scared and sick puppy.

Date _____

Monday
_____
_____
_____
_____

Tuesday
_____
_____
_____
_____

Wednesday
_____
_____
_____
_____

Thursday
_____
_____
_____
_____

Friday
_____
_____
_____
_____

You must take care of your puppy's teeth. Although dogs are less prone to tartar buildup than we are, they aren't immune. Without a little help from us, they'll suffer from tooth decay, cavities, abscesses, periodontal disease, and tooth loss. To keep your puppy's teeth healthy:

✔ Feed your puppy dry food. Crunchy is better.

✔ Start brushing your puppy's teeth once a week. Use a special dog tooth-paste (not human toothpaste) or baking soda. If your dog is averse to the brush, use your finger or a finger brush. If your dog growls, quit immediately and call a professional.

_____

_____

_____

_____

_____

If you have a young puppy, acquaint her with tooth brushing early on. Rub your fingers along her gums throughout the week and praise her calmly as you brush.

_____

_____

_____

_____

_____

_____

_____

_____

_____

Tip of the Week

Some puppies put up an enormous struggle when it's tooth-brushing time. For these critters, your veterinarian will suggest an oral spray that breaks down tartar.

Date _____

Monday
_____
_____
_____
_____

Tuesday
_____
_____
_____
_____

Wednesday
_____
_____
_____
_____

Thursday
_____
_____
_____
_____

Friday
_____
_____
_____
_____

Saturday

Chewing is a puppy thing. It's nothing personal. Puppies don't know a stick from a table leg or a doll's head from a chestnut. Fortunately, they can be rehabilitated. If you have a chewer on your hands, be patient and use some of these tried-and-true techniques. To ward off destructive chewing in the first place:

- ✔ Provide your pup with a supply of appropriate chew toys.
- ✔ Keep the chew toys scattered throughout your home for easy access.

Sunday

Don't yell at your dog after he's got hold of an object. Doing so is bound to make him think it's especially precious. Instead of focusing on the item — or diving after your dog — try to distract him. Shake a treat cup or offer him a toy to attract his attention.

Tip of the Week

If your puppy has destroyed something, kiss it good-bye. Yelling at or hitting your puppy will only make him more nervous and frightened, which leads to more chewing. Remember that your pup just doesn't know any better.

Date _____

Monday
_____
_____
_____
_____

Tuesday
_____
_____
_____
_____

Wednesday
_____
_____
_____
_____

Thursday
_____
_____
_____
_____

Friday
_____
_____
_____
_____

Saturday

Keeping your puppy's eyes as healthy, bright, and clear as possible is up to you.

- ✔ Don't let your puppy hang his head out the car window. It only takes one pebble to knock out an eye.

- ✔ Watch your puppy's head when playing interactive games like stick toss and soccer.

- ✔ If you have a longhaired breed, carefully clip the hair surrounding the eyes.

- ✔ Don't squeeze shampoo onto your dog's head or spray flea repellent directly at your dog's face. Cover her eyes as you apply any products with your fingertips.

_____

_____

_____

Sunday

Does your dog have morning eye crust? It isn't so bad as long as you wipe it clear every day. Use warm water and a soft rag or tissue. Built-up crust can be painful, irritating, and a gruesome sight.

Tip of the Week

If you notice that your puppy's eyes are tearful, full of mucous, swollen, or itchy, see your veterinarian. She may be suffering from conjunctivitis (which is contagious), a cold, internal parasites, or an allergy. If your veterinarian prescribes eye medication, find out how to administer it carefully.

Date _____

Monday

_____
_____
_____
_____

Tuesday

_____
_____
_____
_____

Wednesday

_____
_____
_____
_____

Thursday

_____
_____
_____
_____

Friday

_____
_____
_____
_____

Saturday

Make sure that your puppy is properly identified with a collar and a metal tag with basic ownership information etched on it. You don't want to give too much information away — your home address, for instance. But your name and phone number are essential.

_____

_____

_____

_____

_____

_____

_____

_____

_____

Sunday

You may want to consider some of the following methods of identifying your puppy:

✔ Have a tattoo placed on the inside of your dog's thigh. Use a number that's easy for you to remember.

✔ Have a rice-sized microchip implanted under your dog's skin at the base of his neck When a scaner is passed over you dog, the scanner beeps, revealing a code that identifies the dog.

_____

_____

_____

_____

_____

_____

_____

Tip of the Week

If it's been a month since you last gave your puppy his dose of heartworm medication, now's the time to give him another pill.

Date _____

Monday
_____
_____
_____
_____

Tuesday
_____
_____
_____
_____

Wednesday
_____
_____
_____
_____

Thursday
_____
_____
_____
_____

Friday
_____
_____
_____
_____

Saturday

Be sure to clean your puppy's ears on a regular basis. Using a cotton ball soaked in a veterinarian-recommended solution to help prevent infection, swipe the outer flap of your puppy's ears. Don't go too deep; the ear is tender, and going in too deep can be painful. Repeat this process until the cotton comes up clean.

Sunday

Remember to groom your pup weekly — good habits start early! Choose a comfortable area for you and your pup, and a day of the week that is easiest. Make sure to speak softly to your dog as you brush her and tell her how pretty she is. When you're done, reward her with a treat!

Tip of the Week

Don't use cotton swabs or poke anything else into your puppy's ear canal. You might do irreparable damage.

Date _____

Monday
_____
_____
_____
_____

Tuesday
_____
_____
_____
_____

Wednesday
_____
_____
_____
_____

Thursday
_____
_____
_____
_____

Friday
_____
_____
_____
_____

Saturday

Once your puppy is between 8 and 12 weeks old, you can begin to socialize him. Your puppy still is too young — and vulnerable to illness — for you to take him out on the town. Instead, invite neighbors and friends over, borrow a group of active kids, have a puppy playdate with another healthy canine and socialize that puppy.

_____

_____

_____

_____

_____

_____

_____

_____

_____

Sunday

When your veterinarian has completed your puppy's shots, start taking him out on the town, introducing him to everyone you meet. Take your pup to three new places each week.

_____

_____

_____

_____

_____

_____

_____

_____

_____

Tip of the Week

Veterinarians love a well-behaved dog. It makes their job so much easier. Why not bring your puppy's favorite chew toy with you on veterinary visits? If you have to wait, your puppy's familiar toy will calm him. He may even be too busy chewing to be afraid!

Date _____

Monday

_____
_____
_____
_____

Tuesday

_____
_____
_____
_____

Wednesday

_____
_____
_____
_____

Thursday

_____
_____
_____
_____

Friday

_____
_____
_____
_____

Saturday

The best puppy nail-clipper looks like a guillotine. When you're clipping your puppy's nail, you want to clip the tip, just at the point it starts to curl. Front nails grow faster than hind ones. If your puppy has dewclaws (nails that ride high on the back paws), you'll need to clip them as well. When nails grow too long, they can crack, break, or become ingrown. You'll need to clip your puppy's nails about once a month.

_____

_____

_____

_____

_____

_____

_____

_____

Sunday

Follow these four steps to address the sensitive matter of clipping your puppy's toenails:

1. Initially, just handle your puppy's paws, nothing fancy.

2. Take out some peanut butter and swipe it across the refrigerator at your dog's eye level. As she licks, rub her paws with the clipper.

3. Open and shut the clippers to acquaint her with the sound.

4. Place the edge of the clippers over the top of the nail and squeeze the handle quickly. There — you've clipped a nail!

_____

_____

_____

_____

_____

Tip of the Week

White nails show the nail bed, which you must avoid. If your puppy has dark nails, take extra precautions. If you're concerned, ask your veterinarian or groomer to give you a lesson.

Date _____

Monday

Tuesday

Wednesday

Thursday

Friday

Saturday

If your puppy is just learning to sit, be sure to position him properly but avoid pushing on his spine. With your right hand, gently lift his chin or pull upward on his collar as you squeeze his waist softly with your left thumb and fore-finger. This pressure point tucks him neatly into place without hurting his skeletal system.

Sunday

Start your puppy on a regular training schedule. Keep your lessons short and lively. Sit is always a good place to begin. Use the Sit command whenever you offer your puppy something positive, like food, praise, or a toy. Say "Sit" once, helping your pup into position if he doesn't respond.

Tip of the Week

A treat is a reward, and in most cases, a little goes a long way. Reward your puppy with tiny pieces of hot dog or dried liver. Go ahead and break up a standard treat into smaller pieces for use throughout the day. You want to train your puppy, not fatten him up!

Date _____

Monday

_____
_____
_____
_____

Tuesday

_____
_____
_____
_____

Wednesday

_____
_____
_____
_____

Thursday

_____
_____
_____
_____

Friday

_____
_____
_____
_____

Saturday

Puppies suffering through separation anxiety may chew destructively, soil the house, bark excessively, or act out other destructive behaviors.

To help your pup with her anxiety, try following these ground rules:

- ✔ Leave a radio playing classical music to cover unfamiliar sounds.
- ✔ Place your puppy in a dimly lit area to encourage sleep.
- ✔ Leave a favorite chew toy. Rub it between your hands for scent.

_____

_____

_____

_____

_____

_____

Sunday

A wonderfully distracting treat for puppies is a sterilized bone stuffed with peanut butter. It's a healthy snack, and your puppy will be so busy trying to get at that peanut butter that she'll hardly notice anything else.

_____

_____

_____

_____

_____

_____

_____

Tip of the Week

If you're leaving for more than six hours, find someone to walk your puppy. If necessary, buy an indoor pen. Dogs get cramped and anxious if left in crates or small kennels for longer than six hours at a time.

Date _____

Monday
_____
_____
_____
_____

Tuesday
_____
_____
_____
_____

Wednesday
_____
_____
_____
_____

Thursday
_____
_____
_____
_____

Friday
_____
_____
_____
_____

Saturday

If your puppy seems depressed, excessively tired, or anxious, he may be ill. Before you phone your vet, take your pup's temperature. The temperature of a healthy puppy ranges from 101 to 102.5° Fahrenheit taken with a rectal thermometer.

_____

_____

_____

_____

_____

_____

_____

_____

_____

_____

Sunday

To take your dog's temperature, follow these six steps:

1. Shake down a rectal thermometer until it reads about 95°.

2. Put a dab of petroleum jelly on the tip of the thermometer.

3. Hold the puppy's tail with one hand so that he doesn't sit down.

4. With the other hand, gently insert the thermometer with a slight twisting motion about 1 inch into the rectum.

5. Hold it for at least a minute (three is ideal, but that's a long time to a puppy). Any reading of more than 103° is cause to call the veterinarian.

_____

_____

_____

_____

_____

Tip of the Week

If a month has passed since you last gave your puppy his heartworm pill, it's time for another dose.

Date _____

Monday
_____
_____
_____
_____

Tuesday
_____
_____
_____
_____

Wednesday
_____
_____
_____
_____

Thursday
_____
_____
_____
_____

Friday
_____
_____
_____
_____

Saturday

Keep the following poisonous household items away from your puppy:

- ❑ Household garbage
- ❑ Antifreeze
- ❑ Chocolate
- ❑ Lead
- ❑ Rat poison

_____

_____

_____

_____

_____

_____

_____

Sunday

Plants that are poisonous if ingested by puppies include cactus, dumbcane, tobacco, marijuana, mistletoe, philodendron, poinsettia, azalea bush, daffodil flower bud, honeysuckle, horse chestnut, lily of the valley, morning glory flower, rhododendron shrub, rhubarb, skunk cabbage, tulip bulb, and wild mushroom. Why chance it? Instead, invest in more benevolent blooms.

_____

_____

_____

_____

_____

_____

_____

_____

Tip of the Week

How long has it been since you brushed your puppy's teeth? That long? Healthy teeth are vital to your pup's overall well-being. So get out that toothbrush and establish a regular schedule for your dog so that she can greet you with a gleaming grin for many years to come.

Date _____

Monday
_____
_____
_____
_____

Tuesday
_____
_____
_____
_____

Wednesday
_____
_____
_____
_____

Thursday
_____
_____
_____
_____

Friday
_____
_____
_____
_____

Saturday

Vary your commands so that you aren't constantly saying "No!" to your puppy. When you bring him in from a walk, try saying "Inside." When you don't want your puppy on the couch, use "Off!" If you say "No!" too often, your pup will start to think that's his name. Shouting sounds like barking to a dog. If your puppy thinks you're barking at him, he'll only get more excited.

_____

_____

_____

_____

_____

_____

_____

_____

_____

Sunday

To correct your puppy's behavior, you need to catch him in the act. If you shout "No!" at your puppy after the fact, you aren't communicating anything. If your pup is misbehaving and you can manage to ignore him, the silent treatment is your most effective response. Once your dog stops jumping, encourage him by saying "Get your toy!" and let him pay attention to that.

_____

_____

_____

_____

_____

_____

_____

_____

_____

Tip of the Week

If you don't like to say "No," use another word or sound. Just be consistent. Personally, I like "Ep, Ep." It sounds softer, but the dog gets the message — "Don't even think about it!" — loud and clear.

Date _____

Monday
_____
_____
_____
_____

Tuesday
_____
_____
_____
_____

Wednesday
_____
_____
_____
_____

Thursday
_____
_____
_____
_____

Friday
_____
_____
_____
_____

Saturday

Intestinal upsets are all too common in puppies. These upsets are among the easiest health problems to recognize. If an entire day goes by without your puppy passing stool (or passing watery or bloody stool), she is constipated. Your veterinarian will want to see her if the problem doesn't clear up in 24 to 48 hours. At the onset of diarrhea or loose stools, withhold food (but not water) for a day, but contact your veterinarian immediately.

_____

_____

_____

_____

_____

_____

_____

_____

Sunday

If your dog vomits more than a couple of times, or heaves without ejecting anything more than clear or yellow liquid, get on the phone to the vet.

_____

_____

_____

_____

_____

_____

_____

_____

_____

Tip of the Week

TIP

The most dangerous item for your puppy to accidentally ingest isn't food but rather a piece of cloth or jewelry, or a toy. Such objects can lodge in the intestinal tract and require surgery to remove. Induced vomiting can bring something like a soft latex toy back up. Ask your veterinarian how to do this before your puppy swallows an inedible object.

Date _____

Monday

_____
_____
_____
_____

Tuesday

_____
_____
_____
_____

Wednesday

_____
_____
_____
_____

Thursday

_____
_____
_____
_____

Friday

_____
_____
_____
_____

Saturday

Puppies jump to get their people's attention. Puppies see us as other dogs, and eye contact is a big method of canine communication. Our eyes are above theirs, so to be gracious and greet us properly, puppies think they must jump.

_____

_____

_____

_____

_____

_____

_____

_____

_____

Sunday

The following tips offer some ways to stop your puppy from jumping on you.

- ✔ If your dog jumps on you when you arrive home, ignore him until he's given up the jumping vigil.

- ✔ Keep a basket of balls or squeaky toys by the door. When you walk in, toss one on the floor to refocus your dog's energy.

- ✔ If you crate your dog, don't let him out immediately. Wait until he's calm.

- ✔ Fold your arms across your chest and staring straight up at the ceiling. Do not look down and make eye contact with your pup. Relax this pose only when your puppy has stopped jumping and is calm.

_____

_____

_____

_____

_____

Tip of the Week

If it's been a month since you last gave your puppy his dose of heartworm medication, now's the time to give him another pill.

Date _____

Monday

_____
_____
_____
_____

Tuesday

_____
_____
_____
_____

Wednesday

_____
_____
_____
_____

Thursday

_____
_____
_____
_____

Friday

_____
_____
_____
_____

A neat way to get your puppy to eagerly submit to a bath is by practicing tub exercises well ahead of time. Here's Tub Exercise 1:

1. Say "Tub," and run to the tub. When your puppy joins you, give her a treat. Don't put her in the tub yet. Repeat this a few times.

2. Lay a towel on the bottom of the tub or sink for traction, place some toys around the tub and rub peanut butter on the basin at your puppy's nose level. Don't add water yet.

3. Help your puppy into the tub; then play for five minutes and take her out. Repeat the preceding step once a week until your puppy looks forward to tub togetherness.

_____

_____

_____

_____

Here's Tub Exercise 2:

1. Follow the steps of Tub Exercise 1. Next, run the water as you're playing but let it drain (don't fill up the tub).

2. Once your puppy allows the water to run with her inthe tub, let it fill to hock (ankle) depth. If your dog squirms, stop the water, praise her softly, and offer some treats while you scratch her back lovingly.

3. Put some cotton in your puppy's ears when you bathe her — it keeps water — and germs out!

Proceed gradually until you're able to tub and bathe your puppy peacefully.

_____

_____

_____

_____

Tip of the Week

Stick with one bath a month at most. I never bathe my dogs more than a few times a year, although I do water them down if they need a mud-rinse. The reason? Dogs don't have pores to produce oil. If you bathe them constantly, their coats become dry, dull, full of dandruff, and brittle.

Date _____

Monday
_____
_____
_____
_____

Tuesday
_____
_____
_____
_____

Wednesday
_____
_____
_____
_____

Thursday
_____
_____
_____
_____

Friday
_____
_____
_____
_____

Saturday

Sometimes puppies meet up with skunks, sometimes they roll in dead carcasses . . . yes, I know it's gross — to you and me! But to your puppy? It's heavenly. Here are some tips for avoiding and dealing with those dreadful odors:

✔ To avoid skunks in the first place, keep your puppy on a leash during evening walks (skunks are nocturnal).

✔ Don't bother pouring tomato juice or V8 on your dog — they don't really work. Instead, try a product called Skunk Off. Another option is to rub feminine douche into the dog's fur, which I've heard works wonders.

_____

_____

_____

_____

_____

Sunday

_____

_____

_____

_____

_____

_____

_____

_____

_____

_____

_____

Tip of the Week

When was the last time you took your puppy in for a routine veterinary examination? Check your calendar — it may be time for another visit.

Date _____

Monday
_____
_____
_____
_____

Tuesday
_____
_____
_____
_____

Wednesday
_____
_____
_____
_____

Thursday
_____
_____
_____
_____

Friday
_____
_____
_____
_____

Saturday

If your puppy spends time around children, make sure that she is capable of handling it by acting like a kid. Pull her coat gently, squeal, and make sudden, rapid movements. Praise your puppy and give her treats during your performance.

_____

_____

_____

_____

_____

_____

_____

_____

_____

Sunday

If things between children and puppies get out of control, avoid yelling. To your puppy, yelling sounds like barking and that means fun time. Instead, calmly station, crate, or isolate your puppy until she — and the kids — mellow.

_____

_____

_____

_____

_____

_____

_____

_____

_____

_____

Tip of the Week

Puppy's nails grow quickly — especially the ones on the front paws. But don't forget to keep an eye on all four paws and trim the nails as needed.

Date _____

Monday
_____
_____
_____
_____

Tuesday
_____
_____
_____
_____

Wednesday
_____
_____
_____
_____

Thursday
_____
_____
_____
_____

Friday
_____
_____
_____
_____

Saturday

At approximately 6 months of age, a female dog is ready to be spayed, and a male dog is ready to be neutered. Check with your veterinarian to make sure that your pup is ready for this minor operation. Why spay and neuter?

- ✔ You'll prove that you're a responsible pet owner, preventing any chance of adding to the overpopulation of unwanted dogs.

- ✔ Spayed/neutered dogs live longer, healthier lives than their intact brethren.

_____

_____

_____

_____

_____

_____

_____

Sunday

Ignore the myth that a fixed dog is a fat dog. All dogs that receive adequate exercise and aren't overfed will maintain their girlish or manly figures.

_____

_____

_____

      _____

      _____

      _____

      _____

      _____

      _____

      _____

Tip of the Week

Have you cleaned your pup's ears this week? If you have, I applaud you. If not, it isn't too late! Find that veterinarian-recommended cleanser and gather the rest of your supplies — cotton cloths and treats — and start gently wiping those pointy, droopy, folded, rose-bud, or upright ears. All ears are perfect as long as they're clean!

Date _____

Monday

_____
_____
_____
_____

Tuesday

_____
_____
_____
_____

Wednesday

_____
_____
_____
_____

Thursday

_____
_____
_____
_____

Friday

_____
_____
_____
_____

Saturday

If you discover one flea on your pet, your house probably contains thousands of fleas in various stages of growth. Don't just treat the dog. Although doing so will make her temporarily more comfy, you still need to get rid of the fleas in your house. If you don't, they'll eventually hop back onto your dog — or you!

Sunday

To treat your dog for fleas, you can take him to the vet for a flea dip or spray, or wash him yourself. Make sure to read all labels to see whether the products are guaranteed to be safe for young puppies. If you aren't sure, check with your veterinarian.

Tip of the Week

Keep all flea products away from your puppy's eyes — apply shampoo carefully and never spray a flea product directly at her head or face.

Date _____

Monday

_____
_____
_____
_____

Tuesday

_____
_____
_____
_____

Wednesday

_____
_____
_____
_____

Thursday

_____
_____
_____
_____

Friday

_____
_____
_____
_____

Saturday

Tiny deer ticks carry Lyme disease, which infects dogs and humans alike. Inspect yourself and your dog after every walk. Run a flea comb through your dog's coat after every outing. Ticks take a while to burrow, and a flea comb picks them up.

_____

_____

_____

_____

_____

_____

_____

_____

_____

Sunday

To remove a tick, follow these steps:

1. Stun the tick by applying a cotton ball soaked in mineral oil for 30 seconds.

2. With special tick-removing tweezers you can buy from a pet store, press down on the skin on either side of the tick.

3. Squeeze the skin surrounding the tick tightly and grasp the head.

4. Dispose of the tick in a jar of bleach or vodka. Seal the jar, wrap it in plastic and dispose of it carefully, away from children and pets.

_____

_____

_____

_____

_____

_____

_____

Tip of the Week

Don't spray around your dog's eyes. To treat his forehead and ears, place the product onto a glove and massage in those hard-to-reach areas. Don't forget his paws!

Date _____

Monday
_____
_____
_____
_____

Tuesday
_____
_____
_____
_____

Wednesday
_____
_____
_____
_____

Thursday
_____
_____
_____
_____

Friday
_____
_____
_____
_____

Saturday

Digging is often a puppy's favorite pastime. You cannot teach a dog not to dig. Instead, you must give her a place to dig that's all her own.

- ✔ Pick one area where your puppy can dig to her heart's content, whether it's in your yard or in a local park if you live in an apartment.

- ✔ Go to the same area with your dog each day, instructing her to "Go dig!"

- ✔ If you catch your puppy digging somewhere she shouldn't be, correct her with "No" and then tell her (escorting her to the right spot, if necessary) "Go dig!"

_____
_____
_____
_____
_____
_____

Sunday

_____
_____
_____
_____
_____
_____
_____

Tip of the Week

Most puppies dig if you leave them outside while you're home. They love to dig while you watch; it's a surefire attention-getter. Try to structure your time — and your puppy's time — so that when the urge strikes her, you can dig or play together.

Date _____

Monday
_____
_____
_____
_____

Tuesday
_____
_____
_____
_____

Wednesday
_____
_____
_____
_____

Thursday
_____
_____
_____
_____

Friday
_____
_____
_____
_____

Saturday

Puppies don't like to exercise alone. They need a companion to frolic and play with. Unless you have a couple of dogs, you need to exercise your puppy two to four times a day for about five to 20 minutes each time, depending on his age and breed.

_____

_____

_____

_____

_____

_____

_____

_____

_____

Sunday

Because a walk down the street can be frightening to a new puppy (cars, big dogs, children, and so on), games like those described in Chapter 6 of this book are the best way to exercise your pup.

_____

_____

_____

_____

_____

_____

_____

_____

_____

Tip of the Week

Avoid games like tug-of-war, wrestling, chasing, or teasing, because those games frustrate pups, communicate confrontation, encourage nipping, and make you look like a playmate instead of a leader.

Date _____

Monday

_____
_____
_____
_____

Tuesday

_____
_____
_____
_____

Wednesday

_____
_____
_____
_____

Thursday

_____
_____
_____
_____

Friday

_____
_____
_____
_____

Saturday

The only way to stop your pup from begging for food is to never give in. I know this will be difficult — those big, pleading eyes, the confused expression "You don't want to share that muffin with me?" But begging is a bad habit. It will drive you crazy, it will annoy your guests, it will encourage your dog to bark, and it probably will make her fat.

_____

_____

_____

_____

_____

_____

_____

_____

Sunday

The following are ways to prevent your pup from begging:

✔ Don't allow your puppy in the kitchen while you're preparing food or eating meals. Out of sight, out of mind!

✔ Ask guests not to feed your puppy. You don't want her pouncing on every stranger who walks in the door, trying to nab a free meal.

✔ Make your puppy work for her food. Teach her to sit before you place her bowl down. Ask her to stay until you release her with an "Okay."

_____

_____

_____

_____

_____

Tip of the Week

If it has been a month since you last gave your puppy her heartworm medication, now's the time to give her another pill.

Date _____

Monday

_____
_____
_____
_____

Tuesday

_____
_____
_____
_____

Wednesday

_____
_____
_____
_____

Thursday

_____
_____
_____
_____

Friday

_____
_____
_____
_____

Saturday

Socializing your puppy can be fun. Here are some tips for getting the best results:

- Don't bend to soothe your Scaredy Cat. It reinforces his fearful reaction. Just keep saying to yourself again and again, "Soothing reinforces fear. Soothing reinforces fear."

- Instead of soothing him, try to look confident and stand tall like a good leader puppy. Soon he'll mimic you.

_____

_____

_____

_____

_____

_____

_____

Sunday

Here are some more socialization tips:

- Bring some treats and a favorite toy — something he can focus his attention on.

- Stay calm and positive. Deflect any admirers until he's feeling safe.

_____

_____

_____

_____

_____

_____

_____

_____

_____

Tip of the Week

A great deal of socialization doesn't create a dog who won't protect his home or his people. Socialization simply encourages your puppy to trust your judgment where people are concerned.

Date _____

Monday
_____
_____
_____
_____

Tuesday
_____
_____
_____
_____

Wednesday
_____
_____
_____
_____

Thursday
_____
_____
_____
_____

Friday
_____
_____
_____
_____

Saturday

Puppies like to get in the way. It gets them attention. Whenever your puppy trips you up, gets on the wrong side of the leash, or just basically gets in your way, command "Excuse me" and move her out of your way with the leash or by shuffling your feet gently underneath her belly.

_____

_____

_____

_____

_____

_____

_____

_____

_____

Sunday

When moving your puppy out of the way, do the following:

✔ Don't yell or kick your puppy, and don't use your hands (she'll interpret this as an invitation to play).

✔ Thank your puppy for respecting you; soon, she'll move out of the way with her tail wagging.

_____

_____

_____

_____

_____

_____

_____

Tip of the Week

Check your puppy's girth. You need to be able to see the slight outline of her ribs. If your pup seems too round in the midriff or her ribs are delineated too extremely, you may be feeding her too much, too little, or an incorrectly formulated (for her) food. Be sure to review her diet with your veterinarian.

Date _____

Monday

_____
_____
_____
_____

Tuesday

_____
_____
_____
_____

Wednesday

_____
_____
_____
_____

Thursday

_____
_____
_____
_____

Friday

_____
_____
_____
_____

Saturday

Some dogs like to imitate mules. It's a passive form of resistance. Your dog is hoping that you'll rush back and give her plenty of attention, but don't. Instead, praise the air in front of you and walk a little faster. When your puppy catches up, praise her happily and continue. This method works best with large breeds that have a reputation for being stubborn.

_____

_____

_____

_____

_____

_____

_____

_____

Sunday

If you have a smaller, more delicate breed or a puppy with a timid temperament, kneel down in front of your pup (facing forward) when she puts on the brakes. Tap the floor and encourage her to come to you. When she does, praise her warmly.

_____

_____

_____

_____

Tip of the Week

If you give a stubborn-stopper attention, she's sure to continue stopping whenever she wants a pet, a treat, or your attention. Instead, face forward and proceed.

Date _____

Monday

_____
_____
_____
_____

Tuesday

_____
_____
_____
_____

Wednesday

_____
_____
_____
_____

Thursday

_____
_____
_____
_____

Friday

_____
_____
_____
_____

Saturday

At almost any time between 6 months and a year, adolescence will strike your puppy. That sweet, impressionable little tyke becomes — for a short while — a demanding, disobedient devil. But don't despair. This too shall pass.

_____

_____

_____

_____

_____

_____

_____

_____

_____

Sunday

Here are some tips to help you through puppy puberty:

- ✔ Be consistent, firm, and good-natured.

- ✔ Stand up to your pup and remind her that you're top dog.

- ✔ Keep training sessions short, geared toward the teenaged attention span. Have your puppy briefly sit or stay before going out for walks and before meals. Short sessions also will be easier on you!

- ✔ Use commands one-at-a-time so that your puppy feels good mastering one word before moving on to the next.

_____

_____

_____

_____

_____

Tip of the Week

Your puppy may sometimes act bold and self-assured, but she's still insecure about her world and needs direction from you. Be sure to give her lots of positive attention and don't put too much pressure on her. She's still a baby underneath all that bravado.

Date _____

Monday

_____

_____

_____

_____

Tuesday

_____

_____

_____

_____

Wednesday

_____

_____

_____

_____

Thursday

_____

_____

_____

_____

Friday

_____

_____

_____

_____

Saturday

Puppies sometimes nip when they're upset or anxious. To cure this, you need to find out the reason behind when and why your puppy nips. Is it before meals? Is it when you arrive home at night? Is it when he has to go outside?

_____
_____
_____
_____
_____
_____
_____
_____
_____
_____

Sunday

As you get to know your puppy, you'll be able to read him better. This makes for easier communication and an improved relationship between the two of you. And keep in mind that nipping is a puppy habit. Your adult dog will be less frightened and surer of his place in the hierarchy.

_____
_____
_____
_____
_____
_____
_____
_____
_____
_____

Tip of the Week

If it's been a month since you last gave your puppy his dose of heartworm medication, now's the time to give him another pill.

Date _____

Monday

_____
_____
_____
_____

Tuesday

_____
_____
_____
_____

Wednesday

_____
_____
_____
_____

Thursday

_____
_____
_____
_____

Friday

_____
_____
_____
_____

Saturday

The Wait and Okay commands are wonderful when you and your pup approach unfamiliar or difficult terrain.

First, command "Wait" and bring your puppy behind your feet. This maneuver is best accomplished by taking the leash behind your back. Pause for a couple of seconds and then command "Okay," as you step out first — as the leader, you must always lead.

_____

_____

_____

_____

_____

_____

_____

Sunday

Use Wait and Okay to catch your puppy's attention at doorways, cars, stairs, or before entering an area of high stimulation — the vet's office, a room full of children, or a dog training class.

_____

_____

_____

_____

_____

_____

_____

_____

_____

Tip of the Week

Give your puppy the once-over. Check her coat to make sure that the color is regular. Look into her eyes, clean her ears and brush her teeth. With regular checkups and preventive care, you're sure to have a healthy pet!

Date _____

Monday
_____
_____
_____
_____

Tuesday
_____
_____
_____
_____

Wednesday
_____
_____
_____
_____

Thursday
_____
_____
_____
_____

Friday
_____
_____
_____
_____

Saturday

Taught progressively, the Stay command is a real winner. To prepare for your first lesson:

1. Take your puppy into a quiet room.

2. Slide your puppy's collar high near his head and center it between his ears.

3. First, say "Sit" and align your puppy with your ankles. Then say "Stay" as you flash your hand in front of your puppy's nose; remove this signal and pause for five seconds.

4. Now say "Sit, Stay." This time, pivot to face away from your puppy and pause for ten seconds. Return to your starting point and release your puppy with another "Okay."

_____

_____

_____

Sunday

_____

_____

_____

_____

_____

_____

_____

_____

_____

_____

_____

Tip of the Week

If "Stay!" is your dream command, you're not alone. Some people have trouble with this one because they rush it. Promise me this: You won't rush. Take time with your puppy, and you're sure to see results.

Date _____

Monday
_____
_____
_____
_____

Tuesday
_____
_____
_____
_____

Wednesday
_____
_____
_____
_____

Thursday
_____
_____
_____
_____

Friday
_____
_____
_____
_____

Saturday

Chewing sticks, rocks and socks is perfectly normal. Eating them, however, is dangerous. To distract your puppy from devouring a dangerous — or valuable — object, your first step is to remain calm. Don't dive for the item that your puppy has. Instead, calmly walk away and distract her with a more appropriate object — a chew toy, or a bone.

_____

_____

_____

_____

_____

_____

_____

_____

Sunday

Try these simple tricks to help you divert your puppy's interest in chewing on your shoes and wallet.

- ✔ Place favorite treats in small party cups and distribute them around the house. If your puppy picks up something he shouldn't, encourage him to come to you and exchange the object for the treat.

- ✔ Pick up around the house. If there's nothing to grab, there's nothing to swallow.

_____

_____

_____

_____

_____

_____

_____

Tip of the Week

Never run at your puppy for anything. Racing headlong toward a puppy is scary. Although your puppy may collapse in fear or run from you, she won't learn anything from the experience. Use a treat cup instead!

Date _____

Monday
_____
_____
_____
_____

Tuesday
_____
_____
_____
_____

Wednesday
_____
_____
_____
_____

Thursday
_____
_____
_____
_____

Friday
_____
_____
_____
_____

Saturday

In each room, your puppy needs to have a special corner or area equipped with a bed and a chew bone. Eventually, you want to be able to send your puppy to this area on command — a tactic that is especially useful during mealtime or when you have company.

To teach your puppy this principle, select areas in each room where you want your puppy to settle. Then, with your puppy on leash, command "Settle Down" and point to the area with your free hand.

_____

_____

_____

_____

_____

_____

_____

Sunday

Your puppy probably will need an escort in the beginning. Soon you'll notice that your puppy leads you over and lies down quickly. He may even start to take himself to the area when he's tired. What a good puppy!

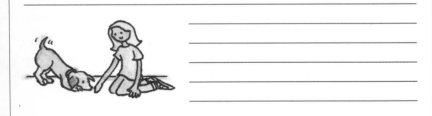

Tip of the Week

Have you clipped your puppy's nails lately? If not, I bet that he needs a trim. So get out those supplies, and snip, snip, snip!

Date _____

Monday

_____
_____
_____
_____

Tuesday

_____
_____
_____
_____

Wednesday

_____
_____
_____
_____

Thursday

_____
_____
_____
_____

Friday

_____
_____
_____
_____

Saturday

The command "Let's Go!" is particularly useful whenever you are walking your puppy on her leash. Remember that "Let's Go!" is not optional. You want your puppy to go, go, go!

_____

_____

_____

_____

_____

_____

_____

_____

_____

_____

Sunday

If your puppy doesn't want to go and you stop to cajole her, you're only reinforcing her resistance. Instead, say the command happily; then skip, bounce or dart ahead — whatever you can do to encourage your puppy's quick and willing participation.

_____

_____

_____

_____

_____

_____

_____

_____

_____

Date _____

Monday
_____
_____
_____
_____

Tuesday
_____
_____
_____
_____

Wednesday
_____
_____
_____
_____

Thursday
_____
_____
_____
_____

Friday
_____
_____
_____
_____

Saturday

Most puppies enjoy learning "Bring" and "Out." Take your puppy into a small, quiet room with a favorite ball or squeak toy and follow these steps:

1. When you bring the toy out, toss it in the air to encourage your puppy's interest; then give it a short toss.

2. If he takes the toy, go to him and say "Good Boy — Out" as you offer him a treat.

3. Continue this process until you notice that your puppy looks to you as soon as he picks up the toy.

4. Gradually encourage him to walk toward you with the toy as you command "Bring." Praise him for releasing.

_____

_____

_____

Sunday

_____

_____

_____

_____

_____

_____

_____

_____

_____

_____

_____

_____

Tip of the Week

Practice these commands in a small room for five days; then bring the commands into normally populated areas, gradually phasing out the treats.

Date _____

Monday

_____
_____
_____
_____

Tuesday

_____
_____
_____
_____

Wednesday

_____
_____
_____
_____

Thursday

_____
_____
_____
_____

Friday

_____
_____
_____
_____

Saturday

The more advanced command "Come!" is a perennial favorite. Try not to overuse it. Don't yell "Come" and run after your puppy, or bribe her with too many treats. Your puppy may think that she's in trouble, or that you're playing a game. And that's no way to get her to listen and come to you.

_____

_____

_____

_____

_____

_____

_____

_____

_____

Sunday

To start training your puppy to come on command, you must get your puppy to come to you when she's already nearby. When you say "Come Front," you want your dog to face you and look up.

1. Walk in front of your puppy while she's standing calmly.

2. Standing tall, say her name and "Come!" Zip your fingers up your belly from her nose level to your eyes.

3. If your puppy looks up but doesn't sit, guide her gently into the proper position. Don't repeat the command while you're getting her to sit.

_____

_____

_____

_____

_____

_____

_____

Tip of the Week

Don't ask your puppy to "Come" when you're mad at her. This will cause her to associate bad things with the command. And then she won't want to come!

Date _____

Monday
_____
_____
_____
_____

Tuesday
_____
_____
_____
_____

Wednesday
_____
_____
_____
_____

Thursday
_____
_____
_____
_____

Friday
_____
_____
_____
_____

Saturday

Remember that a puppy is not a member of the human species, able to articulate angry feelings through words. Dogs communicate through vocal tones, eye contact, and body language. How you cope and redirect this behavior determines how your puppy copes with these feelings as he grows into doghood.

If you bring up your puppy on a play diet of rough wrestling and tug-of-war, he may become aggressive during adolescence. These challenge games often set the stage for later confrontations, which the puppy may not back off from just because you issue the command "No!"

_____

_____

_____

_____

_____

_____

Sunday

If a young puppy is subject to heavy-handed corrections early in his life, he learns self-control through fear, not through understanding. For instance, if you slap your puppy for grabbing a sock, he may grab the sock less when he's with you, but he will be more protective of the sock once he obtains it.

_____

_____

_____

_____

_____

_____

_____

_____

_____

Tip of the Week

If you have a dog who shows aggression, keep him off your bed. This is a big deal! An aggressive dog thinks it's his duty to protect you or keep you in line. The first step in resolving this issue is to take over the high sleeping ground. Station your dog to your dresser for now, if you must. But no bed!

Date _____

Monday
_____
_____
_____
_____

Tuesday
_____
_____
_____
_____

Wednesday
_____
_____
_____
_____

Thursday
_____
_____
_____
_____

Friday
_____
_____
_____
_____

Saturday

The time may come a time when your pup's anal sacs are impacted. You'll know your puppy's anal sacs are irritating her if she frantically tries to bite her tail or lick the area while dragging her backside on the ground. Have your veterinarian show you how to empty these sacs; otherwise, a trip to the vet may be needed about every six months to take care of this problem.

_____
_____
_____
_____
_____
_____
_____
_____
_____

Sunday

If anal sacs are not emptied regularly, infection may occur, and surgery may be required.

_____
_____
_____
_____
_____
_____
_____
_____
_____
_____
_____

Tip of the Week

If it's been one month since you last gave your puppy his heartworm pill, now's the time for another dose.

Date _____

Monday

_____
_____
_____
_____

Tuesday

_____
_____
_____
_____

Wednesday

_____
_____
_____
_____

Thursday

_____
_____
_____
_____

Friday

_____
_____
_____
_____

Saturday

Puppies and children seem to be made for each other, but little kids need to learn how to correctly pick up a puppy. Begin by having your kids sit on the floor and scoop the puppy up into their laps with hands firmly (but gently!) around the pup's mid-section. No one need ever lift or pull a puppy or dog by the front legs. Dogs don't have the same shoulder rotation that people do, and pulling on the front legs can cause irreparable damage.

_____

_____

_____

_____

_____

_____

_____

_____

Sunday

A responsible adult must always supervise dogs and kids. Even if you trust your children implicitly, their friends may be unfamiliar with proper canine care and handling. Don't leave kids and dogs alone together — no matter what!

_____

_____

_____

_____

_____

_____

_____

_____

Tip of the Week

Does your puppy insist on chewing his leash? Try using a spritz of Bitter Apple — on the leash, not on your puppy.

Date _____

Monday
_____
_____
_____
_____

Tuesday
_____
_____
_____
_____

Wednesday
_____
_____
_____
_____

Thursday
_____
_____
_____
_____

Friday
_____
_____
_____
_____

Saturday

You and your puppy can share snacks, but the food you share must be carefully selected. Following is a list of some foods that you can share with your pup. Keep in mind that while these foods may be served either cooked or raw, they must never be served *hot!*

_____

_____

_____

_____

_____

_____

_____

_____

_____

Sunday

Some puppy favorites include apples, cranberries, sweet potatoes, cantaloupe, bananas, berries, broccoli, carrots, string beans, cabbage, corn kernels (off the cob), and eggs (always cooked!).

_____

_____

_____

_____

_____

_____

_____

_____

sit!

Tip of the Week

The foods that you can share with your puppy have one thing in common. Can you guess what it is? Well, let me tell you — these foods are all natural treats courtesy of Mother Nature. Enjoy!

Date _____

Monday

Tuesday

Wednesday

Thursday

Friday

Saturday

Aspirin is not toxic to dogs at doses recommended by a veterinarian; however, it has been known to cause stomach irritation. Buffered or enteric-coated aspirin is better for your puppy.

Sunday

The following painkillers are toxic to dogs:

- ✔ Tylenol
- ✔ Ibuprofen
- ✔ Anaproxen sodium

Never give these to your puppy or dog!

Tip of the Week

Try using the Sit and Stay commands in stressful situations; familiar sounds soothe anxiety — and you'll have a calm, sitting puppy rather than of a frantically pacing one.

Date _____

Monday

Tuesday

Wednesday

Thursday

Friday

Saturday

The command "Stand" is handy when you want to clean muddy paws and during general grooming sessions. Twice a day for four days, take your puppy aside with some treats and do the following:

1. Place one treat between your fingers and give the command as you pull an imaginary string from your puppy's nose forward.

2. When your puppy stands, stop your fingers and cradle her belly as you repeat "Stand."

3. Pause and then release with "Okay" as you allow your puppy to have the treat. Your pup may try to snatch the treat, but hold it firmly and don't release it until she's standing.

4. Repeat these steps five times.

_____
_____
_____

Sunday

_____
_____
_____
_____
_____
_____
_____
_____

_____
_____
_____
_____

Tip of the Week

Have you checked your puppy's smile lately? If not, it may be time to give her pearly whites a nice brushing. Reward her with a treat so that she associates tooth time with good things.

Date _____

Monday

_____
_____
_____
_____

Tuesday

_____
_____
_____
_____

Wednesday

_____
_____
_____
_____

Thursday

_____
_____
_____
_____

Friday

_____
_____
_____
_____

Saturday

Don't let your puppy run free in the house before he's trained. If you permit your puppy to roam freely, he may create havoc in his constant attempt to get your attention.

_____

_____

_____

_____

_____

_____

_____

_____

_____

Sunday

To discourage roaming, I suggest a civilized routine called *anchoring*:

1. With your puppy secured to your side with his leash, slide the end clip up around to your tailbone and sit on the remaining slack of the leash. Make sure that the leash is long enough so that your dog has plenty of room to maneuver — you don't want to choke your pup!

2. Leave enough room for your dog to lie comfortably behind your feet or at your side, and offer him a favorite chew toy.

3. Instruct "Settle down;" pet and praise your puppy when he does so.

_____

_____

_____

_____

_____

_____

Tip of the Week

Avoid dogs and cats with mange, ringworm, or other skin irritations. Make sure that the pets your puppy hangs out with are healthy.

Date _____

Monday
_____
_____
_____
_____

Tuesday
_____
_____
_____
_____

Wednesday
_____
_____
_____
_____

Thursday
_____
_____
_____
_____

Friday
_____
_____
_____

Saturday

An easy, puppy-friendly way to introduce your pooch to new objects is to place treats all around the new item (appliances, furniture — even people!) until your puppy is familiarized and at ease. Remember, puppies "see" things with their noses!

_____

_____

_____

_____

_____

_____

_____

_____

_____

Sunday

_____

_____

_____

_____

_____

_____

_____

_____

Tip of the Week

Vaccines aren't 100-percent guaranteed. Some puppies are allergic to them. Keep your puppy at the animal hospital for a half-hour after initial vaccines and learn the signs and symptoms of each in case she has a reaction.

Date _____

Monday

_____
_____
_____
_____

Tuesday

_____
_____
_____
_____

Wednesday

_____
_____
_____
_____

Thursday

_____
_____
_____
_____

Friday

_____
_____
_____
_____

Saturday

This fun trick is sure to impress your friends and neighbors — and keeps your carpet clean!

1. Take a biscuit, hold it level with your dog's nose, and command "Wipe Your Feet" as you slowly (very slowly!) rotate the treat around his body.

2. Reward half spins initially, then full spins, and then two, three or four spins.

3. Accentuate your hand signals so that soon you won't even need to use words.

4. Eventually, when your dog comes inside with muddy paws, you can point to the foot mat and instruct your dog to wipe his feet — and he will! How great is that?

_____

_____

_____

Sunday

_____

_____

_____

_____

_____

_____

_____

_____

_____

_____

_____

_____

_____

Tip of the Week

If you bend over when giving your puppy a command, don't be surprised if he doesn't listen. You're doing the doggy equivalent of a play bow, a posture that invites a game. When giving your pup directions, stand tall and proud — like a peacock!

Date _____

Monday

_____
_____
_____
_____

Tuesday

_____
_____
_____
_____

Wednesday

_____
_____
_____
_____

Thursday

_____
_____
_____
_____

Friday

_____
_____
_____
_____

Saturday

Curiosity may have killed the cat, but puppies are also stellar snoops. Topical irritants that dogs get into include such things as tar or grease, which can be safely removed by working vegetable or mineral oil into the coat and washing it off with a mild detergent.

_____

_____

_____

_____

_____

_____

_____

_____

_____

Sunday

Only one solution gets rid of oil-based paint on your pup's coat — you'll have to cut away the hair. Never use turpentine, kerosene, nail polish remover or gasoline to remove these substances. Just inhaling such toxic products can be life threatening.

_____

_____

_____

_____

_____

_____

_____

_____

_____

_____

Tip of the Week

If your pup is scratching herself excessively, resist the urge to control her itch with anti-inflammatories. Drugs such as cortisone lower the resistance of the immune system (especially if it's already taxed) and have other side effects. Call your veterinarian for advice.

Date _____

Monday
_____
_____
_____
_____

Tuesday
_____
_____
_____
_____

Wednesday
_____
_____
_____
_____

Thursday
_____
_____
_____
_____

Friday
_____
_____
_____
_____

Saturday

If your puppy loves to stretch, you can turn this penchant into an easy trick, the play bow.

1. As your dog is stretching, bow toward him and say, "Bow!"

2. Praise your puppy as if he invented the dog biscuit.

3. Repeat this scenario each time your puppy stretches. Soon he'll be bowing on cue.

_____
_____
_____
_____
_____
_____
_____

Sunday

_____
_____
_____
_____
_____
_____
_____
_____

Tip of the Week

As your puppy matures, his personality will develop. He'll become a little bit bolder, a little bit braver. He'll march right up to company and demand attention. He'll insist on being at the center of all household activities. Your position as all-knowing leader doesn't impress him as much. But that's okay — your baby is growing up!

Although No Puppy Likes to Visit the Vet, Regular Visits are Recommended!

Initial Office Visit

Veterinarian: _____

    Phone: _____

    Address: _____

    In case of emergency: _____

Puppy's weight: _____

Shots administered: _____

_____

_____

Pills provided: _____

_____

Diagnosis/Special recommendations: _____

_____

_____

Grooming/Nailclipping: _____

_____

_____

Date of next scheduled visit: _____

_____

_____

Notes: _____

_____

_____

_____

_____

Second Office Visit

Veterinarian: _____

Phone: _____

Address: _____

In case of emergency: _____

Puppy's weight: _____

Shots administered: _____

_____

_____

Pills provided: _____

_____

Diagnosis/Special recommendations: _____

_____

_____

Grooming/Nailclipping: _____

_____

_____

Date of next scheduled visit: _____

_____

_____

Notes: _____

_____

_____

_____

_____

Third Office Visit

Veterinarian: _____

Phone: _____

Address: _____

In case of emergency: _____

Puppy's weight: _____

Shots administered: _____

_____

_____

Pills provided: _____

_____

Diagnosis/Special recommendations: _____

_____

_____

Grooming/Nailclipping: _____

_____

_____

Date of next scheduled visit: _____

_____

_____

Notes: _____

_____

_____

_____

_____

Fourth Office Visit

Veterinarian: _____

   Phone: _____

   Address: _____

   In case of emergency: _____

Puppy's weight: _____

Shots administered: _____

_____

_____

Pills provided: _____

_____

Diagnosis/Special recommendations: _____

_____

_____

Grooming/Nailclipping: _____

_____

_____

Date of next scheduled visit: _____

_____

_____

Notes: _____

_____

_____

_____

_____

Fifth Office Visit

Veterinarian: _____

  Phone: _____

  Address: _____

  In case of emergency: _____

Puppy's weight: _____

Shots administered: _____

_____

_____

Pills provided: _____

_____

Diagnosis/Special recommendations: _____

_____

_____

Grooming/Nailclipping: _____

_____

_____

Date of next scheduled visit: _____

_____

_____

Notes: _____

_____

_____

_____

_____

Sixth Office Visit

Veterinarian: _____

Phone: _____

Address: _____

In case of emergency: _____

Puppy's weight: _____

Shots administered: _____

_____

_____

Pills provided: _____

_____

Diagnosis/Special recommendations: _____

_____

_____

Grooming/Nailclipping: _____

_____

_____

Date of next scheduled visit: _____

_____

_____

Notes: _____

_____

_____

_____

_____

Highlights of Your Dog's First Year

_____

_____

_____

_____

_____

_____

_____

_____

_____

_____

_____

_____

_____

_____

_____

_____

_____

_____

_____

_____

_____

_____

_____

_____

Highlights of Your Dog's Second Year

_____

_____

_____

_____

_____

_____

_____

_____

_____

_____

_____

_____

_____

_____

_____

_____

_____

_____

_____

_____

_____

_____

_____

_____

Highlights of Your Dog's Third Year

_____

_____

_____

_____

_____

_____

_____

_____

_____

_____

_____

_____

_____

_____

_____

_____

_____

_____

_____

_____

_____

_____

_____

_____

_____

_____

Highlights of Your Dog's Fourth Year

_____
_____
_____
_____
_____
_____
_____
_____
_____
_____
_____
_____
_____
_____
_____
_____
_____
_____
_____
_____
_____
_____
_____
_____

Highlights of Your Dog's Fifth Year

_____

_____

_____

_____

_____

_____

_____

_____

_____

_____

_____

_____

_____

_____

_____

_____

_____

_____

_____

_____

_____

_____

_____

_____

_____

Highlights of Your Dog's Sixth Year

_____

_____

_____

_____

_____

_____

_____

_____

_____

_____

_____

_____

_____

_____

_____

_____

_____

_____

_____

_____

_____

_____

Part III
The Part of Tens

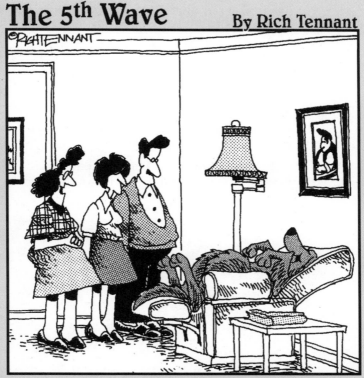

The 5th Wave — By Rich Tennant

"When we got him several years ago he was a Golden Retriever. Now, he's more of a Golden Recliner."

In this part...

Top Ten lists. You can't get through a day without seeing one somewhere — whether it's on TV, at the grocery store check-out lane, or in the morning paper.

In this part, I give you my own Top Ten lists, canine-style: ten ways to keep your puppy healthy and ten of my favorite games.

Chapter 5

Ten Ways to Keep Puppy Healthy

Caring for a puppy is a huge responsibility. However, if you follow the suggestions in this chapter, you're sure to have a well-tended, healthy pup on your hands.

Keeping Puppy Well Fed

Feeding your puppy the wrong diet affects his health and his behavior. The wrong diet can increase your puppy's susceptibility to disease, infection, and possibly nervous/aggressive disorders.

✔ When searching for the right diet, pay close attention to your dog: How's his digestion? Foods with low-quality ingredients don't absorb as well and can give your dog loose stools.

✔ Dry food requires careful storage. If you let it sit around too long, the vitamins may start degrading, or the whole bag may acquire mold or pantry moths.

✔ The need for protein changes throughout your puppy's life and whenever the temperature changes or your puppy suffers from emotional stress. When stress occurs, your puppy uses more protein.

✔ More protein is not necessarily better. High-protein diets are used for show or working dogs. If you have a sworn couch potato or a dog who must spend hours alone, feeding him a high-protein diet (which, broken down, equals energy) makes him jittery and hyper.

✔ Check the nutritional label to ensure you get a blend of high-quality proteins (from dairy and meats) and low-quality protein (from vegetables and grains). A good diet helps your puppy produce two to four compact, inoffensive-smelling stools a day.

Choosing a Good Veterinarian

Choosing a veterinarian is one of the more important decisions of your dog's life (see Figure 5-1). And, unless you live in rural America, you have several to choose from. Following are some concrete guidelines to make finding a good vet easier:

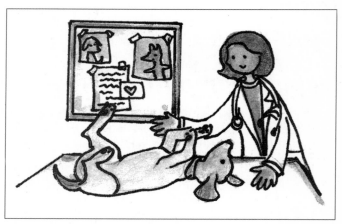

Figure 5-1: Your puppy will need regular vet visits throughout his life.

✔ Ask other pet owners.

✔ Visit the vet with and without your puppy. Call the office first and let them know that you'll be stopping by to check out the place and meet the doctor and staff. When your dog is with you, encourage the staff to feed him. His first recollections will be good.

✔ Look around. Is the environment clean? Well organized? How does it smell?

✔ Ask the doctor some questions. Where did she study? How long has she been practicing? Are there certain diseases she doesn't (or won't) handle? Does she have references for serious ailments or procedures, such as total hip replacement or ultrasound?

✔ Trust your opinion. Do you get good vibes?

✔ Trust your puppy. Does his personality do a 360 when you enter the door? If he's miserable, try a different doctor. If he's still miserable, you'll know that it's all in his head.

Puppies, like kids, need regular checkups. Once you've found a veterinarian you're comfortable with, get out your appointment book and schedule regular visits to ensure that your puppy gets all the protection that he needs.

Making Sure Your Puppy is Properly Vaccinated

First vaccines need to be given as puppies are weaned off their mother's milk. Unless a puppy is orphaned, which requires more medical intervention, a puppy's first vaccine usually is administered at 6 weeks. If a series is recommended, follow-up shots are given two to three weeks later. These shots are called *boosters*. After your puppy reaches doghood, vaccines need to be given annually, in general. Work with your veterinarian to devise a vaccination schedule for your puppy.

Vaccines aren't guaranteed 100 percent. Some dogs are allergic to them. Other antibodies don't build up enough of a defense. Post-vaccine illnesses are tragic. Keep your puppy at the animal hospital for a half-hour after initial vaccines and learn the signs and symptoms of each in case he gets ill.

Checking Routinely for Fleas and Ticks

Nobody wants to think about fleas. However, with a little preventive work and some easy maintenance, you have a good chance of controlling these little pests and keeping your puppy relatively itch free.

Fleas

Contrary to popular belief, fleas don't live on dogs; they feed on them. Fleas live in carpets and grass, so treating the problem involves all-out war. My suggestion? Treat your home the second you discover a flea problem.

- Ask your veterinarian for advice.

- Vacuum, vacuum, vacuum. You not only pick up the adults, but you scoop the eggs and larva from their nests, too. Make sure that you toss the bag after you vacuum, because adult fleas are wonderful acrobats.

- Treat your dog's bedding by washing it with an anti-flea detergent from the pet store or throw it out.

- Talk to your veterinarian or pet care professional about the pros and cons of different products. And don't forget to check the flea product label; it needs to be FDA-approved. Follow the instructions for personal safety.

- Treat all rooms in your house. Fleas love to travel.

- If your home/yard treatment is toxic, make sure that all creatures, two-legged and four, are out of the house for the day (this is a good time to take your pets in for a flea dip).

- Open all windows when you get home; then vacuum again and toss the bag.

- Select a product that treats all life stages (of the flea) and repeat the treatment as suggested.

Yards are tricky and expensive to exterminate. A good freeze takes care of all parties involved, but if you can't wait — or you have mild winters — talk to your veterinarian about your options.

Do not spray, rub, or squeeze flea prevention products near your dog's face or scrotum. Most products are toxic. Talk to your veterinarian first and discuss safe treatments.

Ticks

Ticks are another blood-sucking parasite. Like fleas, ticks prefer furry creatures, but they settle for humans in a pinch. Unfortunately, ticks are found all around the world and can carry airborne diseases.

You can go a long way toward preventing ticks from feasting on you and your dog by:

- ✔ Asking your veterinarian to recommend a tick collar. Secure the collar snugly around your dog's neck. Also ask your veterinarian to recommend a tick repellant.

- ✔ Walking your dog in open sunshine. Ticks love to hang out in shaded, woody areas.

- ✔ Inspecting yourself and your dog after every walk. Run a flea comb, which you can purchase at any pet store, over your dog's coat after every outing. Ticks take a while to burrow, and a flea comb picks them up.

- ✔ Wearing light colors and tucking your pant legs into your socks to protect yourself and wearing a cap to protect your head.

 Killing ticks is hard work. They're drown-proof, squish-proof, and squeeze proof. I find the best way to kill a tick is to burn them or drop them into a jar of bleach, rubbing alcohol, or vodka (for lower toxicity). (Keep the jar out of the reach of the kids.)

Preparing a Puppy First-Aid Kit

Here's a first-aid kit for your puppy. Set these things aside in a safe place or take them with you when you travel with your puppy:

- ✔ Strip of cloth to use as a muzzle
- ✔ Gauze pads

- A sheet or towel that can be used to carry your puppy in a supine position

- A rope or bandana to muzzle your puppy

- A few strips of cloth to tie around a bleeding wound

- A tourniquet rod (use only in severe emergencies)

- Hydrogen peroxide

- The poison hotline number and a list of all poisonous plants

- Bacitracin

- Ice packs

- Snakebite kit if you're in snake country

- Towels to wet in case of heatstroke

- A rectal thermometer

- A towel and water jug (to be kept in your car) in case you get stuck

Please don't take your puppy with you on hot days. A car, even with all the windows down, can overheat within an hour. What a horrible way for a dog to die — locked in a hot automobile, just wanting and waiting for his caretaker to come back.

Getting Puppy Used to Being Groomed

Grooming can be a complete nightmare or a delightful, interactive time with your dog. Whether grooming is a chore or a treat is determined in puppyhood. Keep the first brushing episodes fun and end on a positive note with a treat or a favorite toy.

Following are some suggestions to make your puppy's first associations with grooming pleasant ones:

- Find a soft bristle human/puppy brush. Avoid the wire-bristled brush for now.

- Spread peanut butter or chicken broth in your puppy's food bowl or provide a delectable morsel for distraction.

✔ Make "Tub" a command and practice playing and petting your puppy in the tub long before you give him his first bath. This works so well, your puppy may start jumping into the tub on command.

Stick with one bath a month at most. I never bathe my dogs more than a few times a year, although I water my dogs down if they need a mud-rinse. The reason? Dogs don't have pores to produce oil. If you bathe them constantly, their coats become dry, dull, full of dandruff, and brittle.

Caring for Your Puppy's Eyes

Soulful, sweet, comic — your puppy's eyes express it all. Keeping them healthy, bright, and clear is up to you.

✔ Don't let your puppy hang his head out the car window. Sure, it looks refreshing, but one pebble can knock out an eye. Leave the windows open a crack, if you must, or station your puppy far enough away to keep his face clear of open windows.

✔ Be careful. Watch your puppy's head when playing inter-active games like stick toss and soccer. Eyes are tender.

✔ If you have a longhaired breed, clip the hair surrounding the eyes.

✔ Don't squeeze shampoo onto your dog's head or spray flea repellent directly at your dog's face. Cover his eyes as you apply any products with your fingertips.

✔ Does your dog have morning eye crust? It isn't so bad as long as you wipe it clear everyday. Use warm water and a soft rag or tissue. Built-up crust can be painful, irritating, and a pretty gruesome sight.

If you notice that your puppy's eyes are tearful, full of mucous, swollen or itchy, see your veterinarian. He may be suffering from conjunctivitis (which is contagious), a cold, internal parasites, or an allergy. If your veterinarian prescribes eye medication, learn to administer it carefully.

Caring for Your Puppy's Ears

Dog ears mesmerize me. I can literally lull myself into a trance petting them. And it doesn't seem to matter what shape — uprights, floppy, short, or cropped. Dogs seem to love the ear massage as well. Ah, bliss.

- ✔ Ears need more than massaging to keep them healthy. The ear can play host to all sorts of bacteria, mites, and yeast infections. You must take good care of that flap to prevent these microscopic suckers from moving in and settling down. As a general rule, floppy ears require more care than uprights because air circulation is limited.

- ✔ Clean the outer ear flap. Ask your veterinarian to recommend a commercial ear solution that helps prevent infection. Using a cotton ball soaked in the solution, swipe the outer flap. Don't go too deep; the ear is tender, and going in too deep can be painful. Repeat this process until the cotton comes up clean (see Figure 5-2).

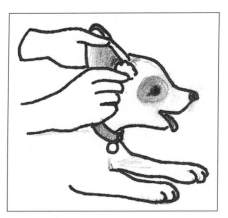

Figure 5-2: Clean your puppy's ears with a cotton ball.

- ✔ Do not use Q-Tips or poke anything into your puppy's ear canal. You can do irreparable damage.

- ✔ Prevent water from entering the ear. If you're bathing your pup, put a large piece of cotton in the opening ahead of time and wipe the ears out with a dry piece when you're finished.

✔ Ear infections are quite common. Signs of infection include a red/swollen ear, discharge, head shaking, ear itching, or a bad odor. What a drag. Get your puppy to her doctor immediately. Left untreated, infections can cause fever, depression irritability and loss of balance. Your veterinarian will prescribe an ointment and teach you how to use it.

Caring for Your Puppy's Teeth

You must take care of your puppy's teeth. Although dogs are less prone to tartar buildup than we are, they're not immune. Sure, they have more concentrated saliva, and they chew bones and things, but this doesn't take the place of proper dental care. To keep your puppy's teeth healthy:

✔ Feed your puppy dry, crunchy food.

✔ Start brushing your puppy's teeth once a week. Use special dog toothpaste. (Avoid human toothpaste; fluoride and dogs don't mix.) If your dog is averse to the brush, use your finger or a finger brush. If your dog growls, quit immediately and call a professional.

✔ If you have a young puppy, acquaint him with this procedure early on. Rub your fingers along his gums throughout the week and praise him calmly as you brush.

✔ As your dog gets older, you may decide to have a yearly professional cleaning. To clean your dog's teeth, your veterinarian needs to anesthetize him; then she scales each tooth separately and finishes with polishing. Good dental care prevents disease and decay.

Some puppies put up an enormous struggle. For these critters, your veterinarian may suggest an oral spray that breaks down tartar.

Clipping Your Puppy's Toenails

The best puppy nail-clipper looks like a guillotine. When you're clipping your puppy's nails, you want to clip the very tip, just at the point it starts to curl (see Figure 5-3). You don't want to cut into the *quick* — the tissue part of the nail.

Aside from being excruciatingly painful to your puppy, the cut will bleed for hours because the quick has lots of veins and nerves.

Front nails grow faster than hind ones. If nails grow too long, they can crack, break, or become ingrown. You need to clip your puppy's nails about once a month.

✔ Initially, just handle your puppy's paws, nothing fancy.

✔ If you're in the car at a red light, turn to your puppy, handle his paws and tell him "Good boy." Have as much hand-on-paw contact as possible for a week or two: no clipping yet.

✔ Next, take out your peanut butter (or broth) and swipe some across the refrigerator at your dog's eye level. As he licks, rub his paws with the clipper.

✔ Don't cut the nails just yet. Open and shut the clippers to acquaint him with the sound.

✔ Now try one cut — just one!

✔ Place the edge of the clippers over the top of the nail and squeeze the handle quickly.

✔ White nails show the nail bed, which you must avoid cutting. If your puppy has dark nails, you need to take extra precaution. If you're concerned, ask your veterinarian or groomer to give you a lesson.

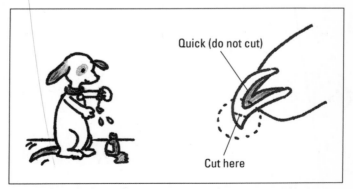

Quick (do not cut)

Cut here

Figure 5-3: Cutting into the tissue part of your puppy's nail will cause the puppy's nail to bleed. Clip the nail at the very tip — where the point starts to curl.

Chapter 6

Ten Fun Games

*P*uppies learn best through play. How you play together, especially in those first few months, influences your relationship more than my mere words can convey. This chapter presents ten (plus a bunch more) games for you to play with your puppy. Read them over, try them out, eliminate what doesn't work, and use them to invent your own. Remember: The games you play with your pup need to encourage cooperation and focus.

Cooperative Games

The games in this section are great for encouraging cooperation and focus, as well as releasing energy.

Soda-Bottle Soccer

This game encourages your dog to follow you and to fetch.

Players: Any number of people and a dog of any age.

To play: Get several plastic bottles (with the caps and labels removed). Place a few on the floor. Let your dog check the bottles out. When she's comfortable, start kicking. No matter how many bottles you have, your dog will want the one you've got. Kick it to her *only* if she's standing calmly (avoid challenging your dog for one bottle; it encourages confrontational play). Then go off and play with another. And so on, and so on, and so on . . .

Rules: Play with your feet, not your hands (it's soccer, after all). Always kick the bottle that your dog isn't chasing.

The Two-Toy Toss

This game helps your dog focus on a variety of toys at one time.

Players: One-dog and one-person team; good for pups older than 10 weeks, although younger pups may show interest for a couple of tosses.

To play: Gather two or more toys or balls. Toss one toy; when your puppy races to get it, cheer her on. As she turns to you, say "Good dog!" and then produce a different toy and start playing with it. When she wants the toy you have (and she will) make sure she sits politely before you toss it.

Rule: Never chase or wrestle a toy out of your dog's mouth.

The Squeak-Toy Shuffle

This game encourages following skills and can be played inside or out. This one is a great diversion for ankle-happy nippers (see Figure 6-1).

Players: One person with one dog; good for pups younger than 12 weeks.

To play: Tie a squeak or rope toy onto a 4-foot leash or line and attach the other end of the line to your shoelace or ankle. Walk around, doing whatever you do. Puppies love to wrestle moving objects: better the toy than you.

Rule: Don't move too quickly or snap the object out of your puppy's mouth.

Figure 6-1: Playing the "Squeak-Toy Shuffle."

Fishing for Fido

Use this game to provide an outlet for chasing instincts and to divert your puppy from attacking your legs. It's great for morning foot-traffic and outside runs.

Players: Good for puppies younger than 12 weeks and their people.

To play: Tie a squeak toy onto a 2- to 5-foot string and attach the other end of the string on a rod (anything passes for a rod: a stick, an umbrella, and so on). Bounce the toy in front of your puppy.

Rules: Let your pup grab the toy often to keep her interested. Avoid tug-of-war. If your puppy insists on tugging, look away until he gets bored; then resume the animation.

The Extended-Rope Toss

This is a great game for releasing energy. The Extended-Rope Toss also helps to relieve predatory energy (better to chase a bottle in a field than a biker on a busy street).

Players: One person, one dog of any age.

To play: Tie an empty soda bottle or favorite toy onto a 20- to 30-foot rope. In a yard or field, swing the bottle around. If there's tall grass, use it as cover.

Rules: Let your puppy run after the soda bottle or toy and grab it. Don't tease him. When he seems to lose interest, reel it in and start all over again. Soon, he'll be waiting for you to toss the toy.

The Treat-Cup Name Game

This game teaches name identification.

Players: Start with two people; then you can add more. Any age dog can play.

To play: Fill a third of a plastic cup with Cheerios or crumbled dog biscuits. Shake the cup until your dog associates the sound with a reward. Stand 6 feet from a friend and, using the other person's name (Jane, for example), tell your dog to "Find Jane!" as you point to Jane. When Jane hears her name, she shakes the cup and calls out your dog's name. When the dog's at Jane's side, Jane can send him back to you.

Rules: As your dog gets better, increase your distance, eventually moving to different rooms and playing outside. Avoid correcting your dog if he loses interest; limiting game time ensures fun.

Hide-and-Seek

Good finding skills lead to good walking and coming skills. You can play this game as an offshoot of the Name Game or just use your dog's name to encourage the find.

Players: One or more persons with a dog older than 14 weeks.

To play: Leave your dog with one person or sitting quietly in a room (if playing alone). Hide (start easy) and shake your treat cup as you call out your dog's name. Praise wildly as your dog gets warmer; quiet down when he's off in the wrong direction.

Rule: Don't make finding you too difficult. If your dog takes more than 30 seconds to find you, you're hiding too well. Quick and easy finds build a dog's determination.

Give (or Drop)

Once you make "Give" less of a demand and more of a direction, your dog will be more likely to share his treasures.

Players: This skill can be taught from the start; it's good for puppies of all ages.

To play: When your dog is chewing on something (whether appropriate or not) approach him with a treat cup (or just a treat from your pocket) and say "Give" as you put the treat in his mouth. (If he's chewing on a dog toy, don't take it away from him.) After your say "Give" and offer the treat, go away calmly. If your dog runs off in fun, practice in a small bathroom. Leave a leash on him around the house to enable a calm catch.

If your dog is growling or clamping the object too tightly, leave it with him until he loses interest and drops it somewhere. Then call a professional. Aggression is no joke.

Take

If your dog loves to carry things in his mouth, you have all you need to teach this game.

Players: Practice this game one-on-one with a puppy who's at least 14 weeks.

To play: Start with a toy or ball and go into a small room or hallway. Wave the object in front of your pup, tempting him for a few seconds before instructing "Take." Cheer when he takes the object, letting him hold on to it for varying amounts of time. Encourage "Give" (using a treat or other toy if necessary).

Rule: Repeat this sequence no more than three times. Always quit while you're ahead.

The Four-Footed Fox

This game encourages interaction and responsibility.

Players: Two people (a sender and a receiver) and a dog older than 6 months old, who's mastered the preceding three games.

To play: Ask your friend (Jane, for example, she's a favorite) to stand 10 feet across the room. Encourage your dog to "Take" a folded newspaper and send her to Jane, saying "Take it to Jane!" Have Jane kneel down and call to your dog. When your dog trots over, Jane rewards him with a treat.

If your dog won't carry the object all the way, have Jane stand right next to you and slowly inch back. With encouragement and love, your dog will become everyone's favorite fax machine.

Rule: Don't discipline your dog if she won't cooperate. This game takes a lot of concentration.

Obedience Games

Who says commands can't be fun? Although you have to be mindful of your tone, mixing lessons into game time can liven up both activities.

Sit, Wait, Down, or Come

This game is a fun way to work on challenging commands like Sit, Wait, Down, or Come (see Figure 6-2).

The players: The person who has trained the puppy. The puppy must be older than 12 weeks and have mastered the command that's introduced.

To play: Pick one command. Race around the room or yard with your dog's favorite toy, stopping periodically to give the chosen command as you lead him into place with the toy. When your dog cooperates, let him have the toy. Get that toy back with a treat by using the Give command, or grab another toy and repeat this sequence five times.

Rules: Don't repeat your commands. If your dog doesn't listen, help him into position before releasing the toy. He'll catch on soon enough.

Figure 6-2: Playing "Sit, Wait, Down, or Come."

Musical Chairs

This game is as much for people as it is for puppies. The puppies have to concentrate on the Stay command around high-level distractions. The people have to stay cool and let go of that competitive edge, or their pup won't be able to stand the pressure.

Players: Any dog who has perfected the Stay command, with at least four dog-person teams, plus an extra person to work the music.

To play: Gather some chairs and a radio/stereo and create a circle. In the center of the circle, place one less chair than the number of people-dog teams playing. When the music starts heel around the outer circle. When the music stops, the dogs must stay as the people move to the center to assume a chair. If a dog breaks the stay, the owner must give up the chair.

The person left out when the music stops is out and must remove a chair from the center. Continue until it's down to two teams and one chair — now the heat is on.

Rules: Avoid getting hyped — your dog won't be able to sit still. Line your dog up toward the middle before instructing "Stay."

Seasonal Fun

No matter where you live, you can take advantage of the great outdoors to interact and bond with your puppy. The following activities are some of my favorites and work great with puppies of all ages.

Winter (for snowbound regions)

Tunneling: Dogs love to dig; what better medium than a pile of snow? Put your mittens on and go tunneling with your dog.

Top of the Hill: After a good storm, the snow piles up. Find a drift or shoveled snow hill and race up it with your dog.

Catch the Snowball: If your dog loves to chase and catch, nothing is cuter than playing with the snow.

Spring

The Great Seed Chase: Springtime bursts with new life. To help spread it around, while amusing your dog, sit on the ground as you pull apart or blow away the seed fragments of various plant life.

Mud Mash: April showers may bring the flowers, but if your dog's a digger, it also brings mud. Rather than getting angry at the holes in the yard, designate a time and a place for digging and take part in the fun. On go the gloves, out with the shovel, and bring some bones to bury.

Morning Dew and the Leaf Tickle: Dogs, like people, enjoy sensations. A dew-drizzled blade of grass and a budding leaf dragged across her nose are just two moments you can share.

Summer

Splash and Fun: Who says baby pools are just for human babies?

The Sprinkler Sashay: If you're a gardener, you're likely to spend a fair amount of time with the hose. While watering your flowers or lawn, you can cool off by playing some obedience games through the sprinkler. Although your dog may resist initially, the refreshing water will win her over.

The Sun Bake: This game is good for either inside or out. Find that sun spot and stretch out with your dog. Let every muscle relax, stroke your dog's ears or the length of her back. Ah . . . the sun can be so soothing.

Fall

The Leaf-Pile Leap: Find a pile of leaves and jump right in.

Hide behind the Leaf Bag: If your dog knows Hide and Seek, all the better. Use your own bags or ones you find in the neighborhood. Hide behind a bag when your dog isn't looking and call out his name. If your dog can't find you, rustle the bag.

Pile the Sticks: If you've got a fireplace, you can actually utilize this game; otherwise, just pile some sticks on a walk. Collect sticks or carry in logs with your dog. Use commands like Carry and Give and thank your dog for helping.

Index

• H •

Sarah
Teaches Dogs, Trains People

arah's PuppyPerfect® Video
earn better by watching? PuppyPerfect is a great way
get the whole family involved.

Patented Teaching Lead
Let Sarah's methods work for you! Her Teaching
Lead brings it all together. It's a humane and
interactive way to train your dog. The **Teaching
Lead Extension** is also available. It adds an
additional six inches to your Teaching Lead, for
dogs and people of all sizes.

Seat Belt Safety Lead
This easy-to-secure lead ensures your dog's safety in
the car. It also doubles nicely as a short leash for
quick control around the house.

- -

ORDER NOW!
Please visit and order on line at **www.dogperfect.com** or send check, money order, or credit card
information to: **Simply Sarah Inc., P.O. Box 420, Bedford Village, NY, 10506.**

arah's Puppy Video . . . .$ 24.95
arah's Training Leash 19.95
he Seat Belt Safety Lead 9.95
AVE! Order All Three for only 49.95
ead Extension 5.00
ubtotal . . . .$____
lease Add:
  Shipping and Handling . . . .$ 4.00
  6.75% New York Sales Tax . . . .$____

My Check/Money Order for $____ is enclosed.
I would like to pay by credit card.
❑ VISA
❑ MASTERCARD
Name on Card: _____
Card #: _____
Expiration Date: _____

our Name: _____

our Dog's Name & Breed _____

ddress: _____

ity: _____ State: _____ Zip Code:_____

mail Address:_____

Visit Sarah's informative website at www.dogperfect.com

FOR DUMMIES

A world of resources to help you grow

Notes